Quilt in a Day®

Christmas
Quilts & Crafts

Eleanor Burns

*For the Quilt in a Day Family, and your
Holiday Spirit throughout the Year!*

Contents

Copyright 1995 Eleanor A. Burns Family Trust

ISBN 0-922705-88-7

First Printing October 1995

Art Direction Merritt Voigtlander
Graphic Artist Susan Sells

Published by Quilt in a Day®, Inc.
1955 Diamond Street,
San Marcos, CA 92069

Introduction

When the days grow shorter and the nights grow longer, a special anticipation begins to take hold. During the fall we have that distant knowledge that December will be filled with celebrating, gift-giving, and entertaining friends and family. Even the scent of a pine cone or peppermint or gingerbread can trigger a planning session! We keep mental lists of what we want to buy, how we will decorate, who will be invited, what recipes to use, and when we need to mail cards and packages.

The Christmas holiday season is my busiest, but favorite time of year. Whirlwinds of thoughts go through my head! Just how will I personalize each gift for those I love?! Then, in December, my sewing machine "smokes": a blue Santa for Cindy to enjoy all year; an extra-extra long quilt to cover Aaron from head to toe; something mauve for Mother.

Decorations are pulled from the attic, gifts wrapped, and holiday china washed. Each year, from the top of a 10 foot ladder, I lament as I stretch across the pine, "Why did I buy such a big tree?" When the tree lights are turned on, casting that warm glow, I know! I just love the season! It's a time when my family and friends gather to share the season of love, joy, and peace.

The Quilt in a Day staff and I have put together this book filled with holiday ideas you can personalize for your family. Even my two sons, Grant and Orion, have gotten into the spirit by contributing to the publication. We've shared the magic of cherished moments plus treasured family recipes. We hope your celebration is more special with these easy projects!

Bring the holidays to your home!

Eleanor Burns

Products

*In Quilt in a Day books we emphasize
using 100% cotton fabrics. Here, we do too,
but there are many other important products used in this book that need to be explained.*

Fabrics

Use 100% cotton fabrics for patchwork. As in quality quiltmaking, 100% cotton fabrics are most satisfactory to cut and sew.

Lamé

If using this lightweight synthetic shiny fabric, purchase lamé that has a backing to give it body and prevent shredding. Use a pressing cloth and cool iron. Lamé is used in the Candle Placemat project.

Fusibles

There are two types of fusible products used to applique pieces. They are very different, so it is important to use the correct one with the method described for each project. Follow the manufacturer's instructions as to heating, steam, and length of time.

Fusible interfacing

This light to medium weight nonwoven film has a smooth surface for drawing on and a reverse side that is rough or dotted that fuses to the foundation piece when ironed. Lightweight fusible interfacing is used in these projects: applique stockings, Poinsettia Wallhanging, and the holly on the Holly Strip Pillow.

Paper backed fusible webbing

The webbing fuses two fabrics together. Use a lightweight brand that has paper on one side for drawing on, and a rough fusible surface that will separate from the paper when ironed onto the wrong side of the fabric and cooled. A medium weight product has a more dense fusing surface that should not be overheated nor edge stitched. Lightweight paper backed fusible webbing is used in these projects: Stained Glass Wreath Wallhanging, Star Catcher Angel, and Wintertime Friends Wallhanging.

Tear Away Stabilizer

This is a nonwoven product used under the foundation when appliqueing pieces to the foundation. Its purpose is to keep the edge stitching smooth. This is particularly recommended when a zigzag or satin stitch is used. It is used in the Stained Glass Wallhanging and Star Catcher Angel.

Glue Guns

A glue gun melts glue and allows you to apply it quickly to a surface for fixing embellishments such as buttons, branches, bows and other bulky items. It is very hot and must be used carefully to avoid burns and dripping glue. Keep a bowl of cold water beside you if hot glue should drip on your skin. A safer tool is the low temperature glue gun, popular for children and adults to use.

Applique Tools

A wide **straw** and **bodkin** are used to turn small sewn pieces right  side out. Cut a slit in the backing or interfacing, insert the straw toward an end point and gently poke the end point into the straw. Remove the straw and finish turning the piece right side out.

The "point" end of the **point turner and seam creaser** serves the purposes of poking out the corners and points of turned pieces. The "creaser" end is used to flatten pieces once they are turned right side out.

The **"wooden iron"** is a wood tool with a flat edge used to crease seams flat.

Battings

The general category of battings include what is used as the middle layer of quilts, placemats and table runners; stuffing for decorations; as well as the back and/or front of other decorations. These products might be sold in packages, on the bolt, or in wide widths. The composition ranges from 100% polyester to 100% cotton. The density ranges from fluffy to firm. Some polyester products would melt if ironed while other polyester products are designed to be fused in clothing and crafts.

In order to choose the right product for your project, compare the use of the project with the manufacturer's recommendations. For instance a lightweight polyester quilt batting in a project might melt if ironed, while another polyester product is designed for fusing with fabric. A dense fleece-like product is used in the Candle Placemats and Pine Tree Table Runner.

A dense cotton batting is important if used as the sturdy outside layer of a stuffed project, but use 100% polyester in order to shred it and poke it inside. Stuffed projects are the Snowman, Angel and Nicholas.

Choose a thin, lightweight batting for the middle layer of quilts that will be machine or hand quilted. This is usually described as 2 to 5 oz. weight. A thicker, fluffier polyester batting is used for tying quilts, and is usually described as 8 to 20 oz. weight.

General Techniques

Materials Chart

The project Materials Charts show how much yardage is needed of each fabric. *If very little is required, only the measurements are listed.*

The listed yardage is further described by indentation in how many pieces or strips to cut.

A further indentation indicates how that piece or strip is cut into smaller pieces.

Example of Pine Tree Materials Chart

Tree green
½ yd
     7½" wide strip
          five 7½" squares

Cutting Straight Strips

1. Make a nick on the selvage edge, and tear your fabric from selvage to selvage to put the fabric on the straight of the grain.

2. Fold the fabric in half, matching the torn straight edge thread to thread.

3. With the fold of the fabric at the bottom, line up the torn edge of fabric on the gridded cutting mat with the left edge extended slightly to the left of zero. Reverse this procedure if you are left-handed.

4. Line up the 6" x 24" ruler on zero. Spread the fingers of your left hand to hold the ruler firmly. With the rotary cutter in your right hand, begin cutting with the blade off the fabric on the mat. Put all your strength into the rotary cutter as you cut away from you, and trim the torn, ragged edge.

5. Lift, and move the ruler over until it lines up with the desired strip width on the grid and cut. Accuracy is important.

6. Open the first strip to see if it is straight. Check periodically. Make a straightening cut when necessary.

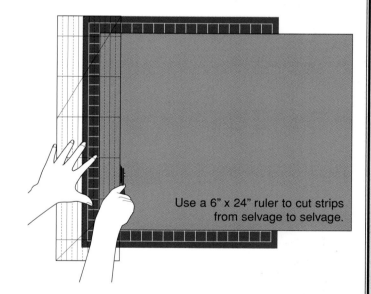

Use a 6" x 24" ruler to cut strips from selvage to selvage.

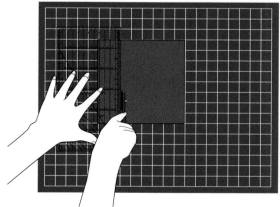

Use a 6" x 12" ruler to cut shorter strips and smaller pieces.

Using Square Rulers

Cut a number of squares the same size.

1. Cut a long strip at that measurement.
2. Use a square ruler to cut squares from that strip.

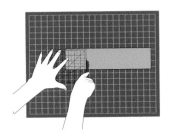

Use a 12½" Square Up ruler to cut large squares and rectangles. Use a 6" x 6" ruler to cut small squares and rectangles.

1. Place the ruler on the fabric with the 1" ruler mark in the upper right hand corner.
2. Cut a slightly larger piece with the grain of the fabric.
3. Turn the piece, and cut to exact size.

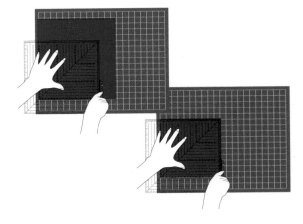

Sewing

Stitch size

Use a small stitch, 12 to 15 to the inch or a setting of 2.

¼" seam allowance

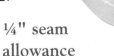

Use a consistent ¼" seam allowance throughout construction. Fabric fed under the presser foot at its right edge isn't necessarily a ¼". Make a test sample and measure the seam allowance. If necessary, adjust the needle position, change the presser foot, or feed the fabric under the presser foot to achieve the ¼".

A magnetic seam guide placed at the right of the presser foot will assure a consistent seam allowance.

Use a gridded pressing mat to help keep long pieces pressed straight.

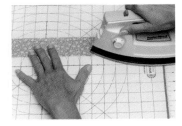

To "set the seam," lay a closed sewn pair of strips (or other pieces) on the mat. Press the stitching.

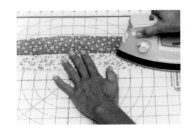

To "direct the seam allowance," lift the upper piece and press toward the seam. The seam allowance naturally falls behind the upper piece. Make sure there are no folds at the seam line.

Projects Children Can Make

Many of the projects in the book can be made by children with some sewing and craft experience. And some are easy enough for a beginner.

How to choose a project

Since you know what your child is capable of tackling, carefully look through the book and read the ones that are possibilities. Ask yourself questions like these…

- Is it easy enough?
- What tools can he/she use safely?
- How much adult help is necessary?
- Do we have the supplies on hand, or where can we pick them up?
- Will we have enough uninterrupted time to work together?
- Will the child have fun?

Among the easiest, consider…

Strip Holly Pillow

Angel Ornament

Yo yo Tree

Stuffed Snowman

With some experience, consider…

Tree Shirt

Stuffed Angel

Hints:

- 100% cotton fabric for the Strip Pillow may be torn instead of rotary cut.
- Low temperature glue guns are safer than hot glue guns.
- Stuffing may be purchased in bags, or may be shredded from polyester quilt batting.
- A youngster's confidence and self-esteem grows when a project is finished successfully. And it doesn't have to be perfect! When you praise the effort that went into it, your compliments are directed toward the maker. The glow of satisfaction often outshines any imperfections.

Sing-a-long to the tune of Santa Claus is Coming to Town

by Mackie

Mackie

Here at Q I A D we want you to know
We never say "rip," we call it "unsew."
Eleanor is sewing today.

She's making a pocket for her rotary blade,
would you look at all the last minute gifts that she's made.
Her Elna is smoking away!

She's made a patchwork Santa,
Out of antique quilts, you know.
He stands there with his arms out,
But he never says, "ho-ho."

So, if you have a last minute gift you must give,
Don't go to the store, make one that will live.

A gift made with love from you, will last a lifetime thru'.

Happy Birthday Jesus

Christmas! Once again, our home is filled with the wonderful aroma of an evergreen forest.

Decorations go up, lights sparkle, and stockings are hung. Cards and letters arrive from friends and family, telling about the past year's events. Our family, separated by too many miles, is together again.

All of these things make up Christmas, but how do we impress upon our young children what Christmas really is?

Kids love a birthday party, so we have one for the King! Complete with cake, decorated in birthday fashion, the candles are lit, and the song is sung. Happy birthday, dear Jesus, happy birthday to you!

"And the angel said to them, be not afraid: for behold, I bring you good news of a great joy which will come to all the people; for unto you is born this day in the city of David a Savior, who is Christ the Lord." Luke 2:10-11

Happy Birthday Jesus. Thank you for coming.

Linda Dallman

Fanciful Holiday Friends

Sue Bouchard

"Old Quilt Fabric"

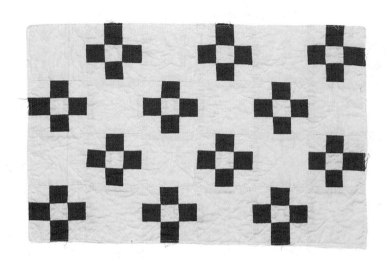

$\mathcal{T}$he following technique is used to create a piece of textured and colored fabric which looks as though it were cut from an old quilt. The Snowman and Angel use the same size "old fabric" while Nicholas uses a larger piece.

Because red often "bleeds," separately pre-wash the red and white fabrics. Do not pre-wash the flannel and muslin. After the patchwork is made, layered with flannel and muslin backing and machine quilted, wash and dry it twice to shrink for an antique texture.

Materials   Cut strips selvage to selvage.

12" x 18" "old quilt" for Angel and Snowman

Red, pre-wash
  ⅛ yd
      two 1½" wide strips
          Cut one strip in half

White, pre-wash
  ½ yd
      three 1½" wide strips
          Cut one strip in half
      3½" strip into:
          twelve 3½" squares

White or Beige Flannel, do not pre-wash
  ½ yd
      16" x 22" piece

Muslin, do not pre-wash
  ½ yd
      16" x 22" piece

27" x 36" "old quilt" for Nicholas

Red, pre-wash
  ½ yd
      eight 1½" wide strips

White, pre-wash
  1 yd
      ten 1½" wide strips
      five 3½" strips into:
          (54) 3½" squares

White or Beige Flannel, do not pre-wash
  ⅞ yd
      31" x 40" piece

Muslin, do not pre-wash
  ⅞ yd
      31" x 40" piece

Instructions

Making Nine-Patches

Twelve for Angel and Snowman

Fifty-four for Nicholas

1. Stack and lay out 1½" strips each of white, red, white.

   Angel and Snowman: one in each stack

   Nicholas: four in each stack

2. Use ¼" seam allowance and 15 stitches to the inch. Assembly-line sew.

3. Press seam allowances to the red fabric. Set aside.

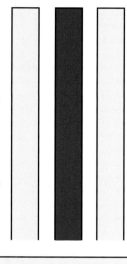

4. Lay out strips of red, white, red.

   Angel and Snowman: half in each stack

   Nicholas: two in each stack

5. Sew sets.

6. Press seam allowances to the red fabric.

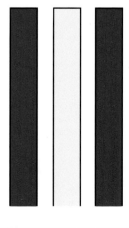

7. Cut 1½" pieces from each set of strips.

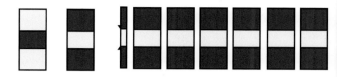

8. Lay out pieces in stacks. Place this many in each stack:

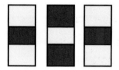

   Angel and Snowman: Twelve

   Nicholas: Fifty-four

9. Assembly-line sew Nine-Patches, matching the seams.

10. Press seam allowances away from center.

Sewing the "Old Quilt" Fabric

Squares should be same size as Nine-Patch.

1. Lay out the stacks of Nine-Patches and 3½" white squares.

2. Flip the Nine-Patch to the square, right sides together. Assembly-line sew.

3. Press seam allowance to the square.

4. Lay out the stacks of pairs.

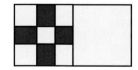 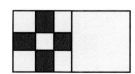

5. Assembly-line sew.

6. Lay out the sewn rows in alternating directions.

   Angel & Snowman: 4 blocks x 6 blocks

   Nicholas: 9 blocks x 12 blocks

7. Sew the rows together.

Example of 4 blocks by 6 blocks

Quilting the Patchwork Fabric

1. Mark your quilting pattern diagonally across each square.

2. Layer the patchwork to the flannel and muslin backing.

3. Pin the three layers together.

4. Machine quilt with invisible or regular thread, about 8 to 10 stitches to the inch.

5. Machine baste around the outside edge to avoid fraying.

6. Machine wash and dry twice for an old fashioned texture.

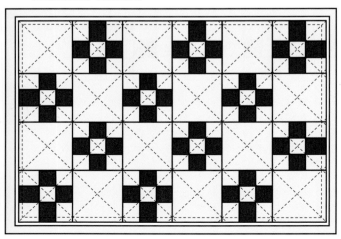

Antiquing the Fabric

To simulate the coloration of an old quilt, choose between these methods:

   Purchase a cold water tea dye

   Make your own dye

Making Your Own Dye

Make your own solution using any store brand instant tea or instant coffee, without lemon or sugar.

1. In a bowl large enough to hold the patchwork, dissolve 2 - 3 tablespoons of instant tea or coffee in tepid water. Use more granules if not dark enough.

2. Dip patchwork and remove. If darker color is desired, leave in longer. Blot out excess moisture with paper towels.

3. Set the color by drying in the sun or drying in dryer.

4. If you choose to iron the prepared fabric, lay it between pressing cloths to prevent scorching and discoloring ironing board cover.

Strufoli

2 cups sifted all-purpose flour

3 eggs

¼ tsp salt

½ tsp vanilla extract

Set out deep saucepan or automatic deep-fryer for deep-frying and heat fat to 365 degrees.

Meanwhile, place sifted all purpose flour and salt into a large bowl. Make a well in center of flour. Add eggs, one at a time, mixing slightly after each addition. Add vanilla extract. Mix well to make a soft dough.

Turn dough onto a lightly floured surface and knead. Divide dough into halves. Lightly roll each half ¼" thick to form a rectangle. Cut dough with a pastry cutter into strips ¼" wide. Use palm of hand to roll strips to pencil thickness. Cut into pieces about ¼" to ½" long.

Fry only as many pieces of dough as will float uncrowded, one layer deep in the fat. Fry 3 to 5 minutes, or until lightly browned, turning occasionally during frying time. Drain over fat before removing to absorbent paper.

1 cup honey

1 tbs tiny multicolored candies

1 tbs sugar

Meanwhile, cook honey and suger in skillet over low heat about 5 minutes. Remove from heat and add deep-fried pieces. Stir constantly until all pieces are coated with honey-sugar mixture. Remove Strufoli with a slotted spoon and set in refrigerator to chill slightly. Remove to a large serving platter and arrange in a cone-shape mound. Sprinkle with multicolored candies.

Chill in refrigerator. Serve by breaking off individual pieces. 8 to 10 servings.

Diana Rivera

Arrange these tiny balls—deep fried and honey-coated—in a cone and cluster shapes to be used as a center piece on Christmas Day.

Stuffed Angel

Eleanor Burns

*L*et your spirits take wing this holiday season with these delightful angels fashioned from bits and pieces of memorabilia. She is heavenly robed in a country gown from a recycled quilt, or Victorian in a dresser scarf trimmed with ribbons. It's easy to turn your treasured doilies, ribbons, laces, and flowers from your stash into an Angel you can cherish throughout the year. The construction is so simple, children can delight in making one. Instructions for making an "old quilt" are on page 12.

Angel size: 14"
Pattern provided

Materials

Dress and arms
12" x 18" "Old Quilt" piece or dresser scarf

Head and hands
5" x 8"

Wings
two 6" x 12"
6" x 12" fusible fleece

Lining
½ yd muslin

Other Materials

stuffing (shredded polyester batting)

batting scraps

1 yd ¼" ribbon

black permanent marker

blush

chopstick for turning

hot glue gun

Spanish moss

3" grape ivy wreath

silk or dried flowers

4" doily

Instructions

Cut these Pieces

Quilt or dress scarf - one dress, one arm
Lining - one arm
One head
One hand (2½" x 4")

Making the Body

1. Trace eyes on head with permanent marker.

2. Sew head to dress with a ¼" seam allowance. Use 15 stitches per inch for thin layers of muslin. Use 10 stitches per inch for quilted layers.

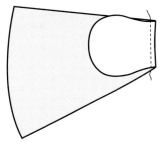

3. Pin body right sides together to piece of lining. *Optional:* Place light batting underneath. Cut around shape.

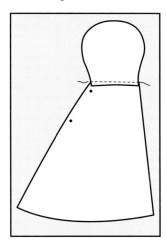

4. Sew around the outside edge, leaving an opening between dots on body.

5. Trim, and turn right side out.

6. Stuff firmly with layers of thick batting cut to size or shredded batting. Slipstitch opening shut.

Making the Wings

1. Iron fusible fleece to wrong side of fabric.

2. Place fabric right sides together with pattern on top. Cut out wings.

3. Stitch around the outside edge, leaving open between dots.

4. Trim and turn. Slipstitch opening shut.

5. Edge stitch.

Making the Arms

1. Sew hand to arm. Flip back to cover arm piece.

2. Place lining and arm right sides together.

3. Stitch around the outside edge, leaving opening between dots.

4. Trim and turn.

5. Stuff lightly on the ends. Do not stuff in the center.

6. Slipstitch the opening shut.

7. With a double strand of thread and hand sewing needle, gather the center of the arms.

8. Wrap around the body and hot glue the "hands" together.

Finishing the Angel

1. "Blush" the cheeks.

2. Hot glue Spanish moss for hair.

3. Hot glue on wings, bow and other embellishments. Make a "nosegay" by gluing flowers in the doily.

Suggestion: Use Angel to decorate a 24" wreath.

Stuffed Snowman

Sue Bouchard

Snowman size: 10" x 16"
Pattern provided

*S*everal years ago my Aunt Betty was making snowmen from old "cutter" quilts. Now you can make your own stuffed snowman from a quilt you might have which is beyond repair, or from fabric you patch yourself with flannel and wash to make look old. Another option is to use an old chenille bedspread to give your snowman an even softer look. The snowman is then embellished with a hat, carrot nose and other trinkets to look just like the ones the children decorate. Instructions for making the "old quilt" is on page 12.

Materials

Make the snowman with an "old quilt" or chenille front, and back with 100% cotton batting, or make both front and back from 100% cotton batting.

Snowman front
11" x 16" "old quilt," chenille, or firm 100% cotton batting

Snowman back
11" x 16" firm 100% cotton batting

Scarf
1¼" x 18" piece

Hat
black sock

Face
two ⅜" (9 mm) buttons
1½" "carrot"

Embroidery Floss (handsewing)
ecru and black

Polyester batting scraps for stuffing

Other Materials (optional)

sticks for arms

string of craft "lights"

3" basket

artificial pine

pine cone

buttons

bell or pompom

Instructions

Making the Stuffed Snowman

1. Layer the front on the cotton batting. *Place "old quilt" right side up, and chenille right side down.*

2. Place the pattern on top and pin.

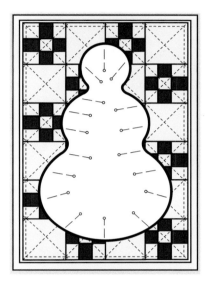

3. Sew around the outside edge:

Old Quilt or Batting Snowman

By Hand: Cut around pattern. Using the embroidery floss, sew a straight stitch or blanket stitch. Leave a hole for stuffing.

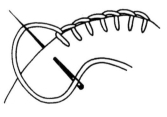

By Machine: Draw around the pattern, and sew on the line with a straight stitch or blanket stitch. Cut after the stitching is completed.

Chenille Snowman

Cut ¼" away from pattern to allow for seam. Sew around the outside edge, leaving an opening in the bottom. Turn and stuff.

Arms: "Rip" out a few stitches in the seam. Insert sticks, and hot glue in place.

4. Hot glue embellishments in place.

Making the Hat

1. Cut 6" off the cuff of a sock.

2. Fold cut edge in half, and stitch.

3. Turn right side out.

   Optional: Decorate with a button, bell or pompom.

Antiquing Cotton Batting

1. Fill a spray bottle with cold water.

2. Add a tablespoon of instant tea or coffee. Mix.

3. Lightly spray on the batting and let dry.

Nicholas

Eleanor Burns

$\mathcal{E}$ven though the image and legend of Nicholas has changed from country to country, he has brightened the lives of children in the world for over a thousand years. Whether you make his priestly robe from a recycled old quilt, or your own "old quilt," or fashion it from new fabric, Nicholas will brighten your holidays. Instructions for making the "old quilt" are on page 12.

Nicholas height: 22"
Pattern provided

Materials

Muslin body
¾ yd

Coat and hat
¾ yd coat fabric
¾ yd lining fabric
or "old quilt piece" - 27" x 36"

Mittens
4½" x 12"

Knapsack - burlap or coat and lining fabric
two 7½" x 11"
24" drawstring

Other Materials

stuffing
soft 100% polyester batting scraps or
1# bag of stuffing

whiskers and hair
natural sheep fleece

face
blush make-up

eyes
two ¼" (7 mm) buttons or black
laundry marker

base of body
4" x 5½" x 2" piece of pine or Douglas fir

hot glue gun

Optional Decorations

3" grapevine wreath

¼" ribbon

buttons

cording for belt

fur

pine, pine cones

small toys

2½" glasses

Instructions

Making the Body

1. Place pattern pieces on muslin. (If you cut carefully, you may get enough for two bodies from the ¾ yd.)

2. Layer cut two fronts, and one back.

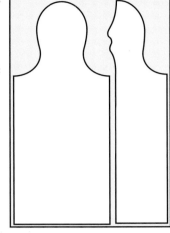

3. Sew front center seam right sides together.

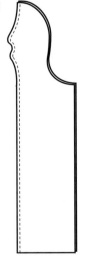

4. Match and pin front to back. Sew around outside edge, leaving bottom open.

5. Turn right side out.

6. Shred the batting into soft lumps. Stuff nose and chin with round ball of batting. Stuff body firmly to 2" from bottom.

7. Fold edge under 1", and staple or tack to block of pine. Take tucks if necessary.

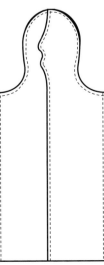

Making the "Old Quilt" Coat

1. Layer cut two coats on the fold. Clip at the neckline.

2. With right sides together, sew from clip to end of sleeve.

3. Sew side seams.

4. Slip onto the body, and lightly stuff shoulders and arms. Roll up cuffs.

Making the Lined Coat

1. Fold fabric in half so piece is 13" x 22". Layer cut two coats on the fold from each fabric. Clip at neckline.

2. Separately sew shoulder seams on coat and lining. Press open.

3. Place coat and lining right sides together. Pin and sew cuffs and bottom edges together. Turn right side out.

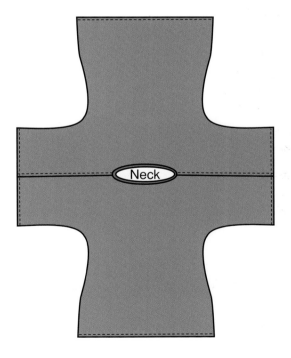

Neck

4. Fold coat right sides together.

5. Pin one coat underarm seam right sides together.

6. From opposite side, reach hand through center of coat, pull pinned coat seam back through and stitch in a "circle" around coat and lining. Turn right side out.

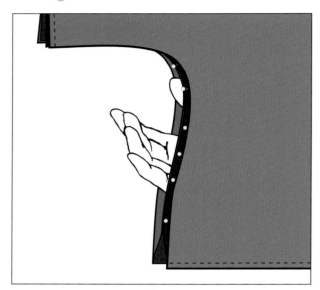

7. Pin edges of lining right sides together near bottom of coat. Begin on the lining and sew toward the coat. Keep turning fabric, sewing in a "circle." Leave a 3" hole for turning.

Sew toward coat

8. Pull right side out.

9. Slip onto body, and lightly stuff shoulder and arms. Roll up cuffs.

10. Fold under neck edge and stitch to body. (Optional)

Making the Mittens

1. Fold right sides together into fourths. Layer cut four.

2. Stitch pairs, right sides together, around the curved edge with ¼" seam, 20 stitches per inch, and thread to match. Leave straight end open.

3. Turn right side out, and firmly stuff.

4. Insert in end of sleeve, and hot glue in place.

Making the Lined Hat

It is not necessary to line the "old quilt" hat.

1. Layer cut two each from the "old quilt," and coat and lining fabric.

2. Right sides together, sew back seam and turn right side out.

   To line Hat: Turn hat only right side out. Place hat right sides together to lining. Stitch around outside edge, leaving a small hole on bottom for turning.

3. Position on head, and stuff lightly.

Making the Face

1. Add blush to cheeks. Make dots for eyes or sew on buttons.

2. Hot glue hair, whiskers, mustache and eyebrows.

3. Hot glue hat in place, and fold back cuff.

Making the Lined Knapsack

It is not necessary to line an "old quilt" or burlap bag.

1. With knapsack and lining right sides together, sew the 11" side.

2. Open, and fold in half the opposite way with right sides together.

3. Sew around the outside edge, leaving a small opening in the lining.

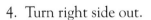

4. Turn right side out.

5. Fold over 1" casing and stitch. Pull drawstring through.

6. Fill with batting and decorations. Hot glue in place over the shoulder.

Finishing Touches

1. Wrap cording around Nicholas' middle.

2. Embellish with glasses, buttons, fur, pine, tiny pieces of toys or fruit, twigs, a small flag, or piece of quilt.

Chocolate Cherry Cake

1 package of chocolate cake mix (dry)

3 eggs

1 large can of cherry pie filling

Mix all of the ingredients together with an electric mixer. Follow box suggestions for pan size. Bake at 350 degrees 35 to 40 minutes. Frost with chocolate fudge frosting.

Anne Cann

For our family the holidays are a special time of reflection on the faithfulness of God throughout the year. Just as the recipe for the Chocolate Cherry Cake is rich to the taste, so is the mercy of the Lord.

Anne Dease   Patricia Knoechel

Wintertime Friends

*N*othing says winter more than the sight of Christmas trees and a friendly snowman greeting the season with his frosty smile. This easy-to-piece quilt will add some holiday fun to your home. Using 100% cotton batting to make your fusible snowmen adds wonderful texture and fuzziness to your frozen friends!

Wallquilt size: 31" square
Pattern provided

Materials   Cut strips selvage to selvage.

Dark sky background (snowmen)
> ¼ yd
>> 7½" wide strip
>>> five 7½" squares

Light sky background (trees) and light border
> ¾ yd
>> 7½" wide strip
>>> four 7½" squares
>> three 3½" wide strips

Tree
> ¼ yd

Tree trunk
> 2" x 5"

All cotton batting for snowmen
(polyester batting won't withstand ironing of fusible webbing)
> 15" square

Folded border, at least 44" wide and binding
> ½ yd
>> two 1¼" wide strips
>> three 3" wide strips

Pieced squares border, 5 different medium to dark
> ⅛ yd of each
>> 2½" wide strip of each

Paper backed fusible webbing
> ½ yd

Backing and hanging sleeve
> 1⅛ yds
>> 36" square
>> 4" wide strip

Bonded batting
> 34" square

Other Materials

> neutral sewing thread
>
> black thread for blanket stitch
> (optional: embroidery floss for handwork)
>
> medium tip black permanent ink pen
>
> ten ⅜" (9mm) black buttons for snowmen
>
> scraps for snowman scarves, ¾" x 5" each
>
> glue gun

Embellishments

> star buttons for tree tops
>
> pearls for snow
>
> craft strings of ornaments, string pearls
> or rick-rack

Instructions

Making the Appliqued Trees and Snowmen

1. Make template and trace four trees and five snowman patterns onto paper side of fusible web.

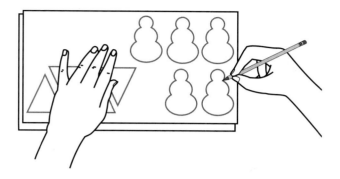

2. Press traced trees design onto wrong side of the tree fabric. Use a hot, dry iron or follow the manufacturer's directions.

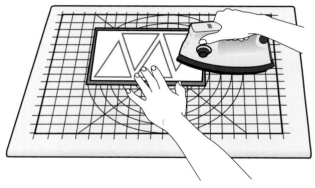

3. Press traced snowman design onto the all cotton batting (wrong side if there is a wrong side or all-white side). Do not use polyester batting.

4. Press a 2" x 5" strip of paper backed fusible webbing on the wrong side of the trunk fabric. Cut four 1" x 1¼" tree trunks.

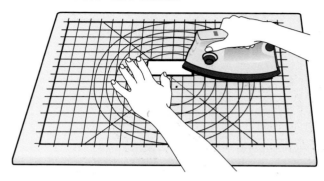

5. Cut out design on drawn lines. Peel off paper from webbing.

6. Center trees and trunks on 7½" light background.

   Center snowmen on 7½" dark background.

7. Press to secure applique. Use hot, dry iron or follow the manufacturer's directions.

8. Blanket stitch around appliques. Optional: use zigzag or satin stitch.

9. Draw in smile and eyes with permanent marker for snowman face, or handstitch if preferred.

10. If hand sewing pearls and buttons, add them now. Otherwise, glue on after quilt is completed.

Sewing the Nine-Patch

1. Lay out the nine squares.

2. Flip the middle row to the left, and assembly-line sew vertical seam.

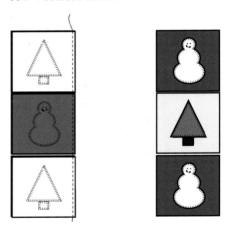

3. Open and assembly-line sew the right row.
4. Sew the horizontal seams.
5. Press.

Adding the Folded Border

1. Fold lengthwise wrong sides together and press the 1¼" wide folded border strips. Cut in half to make all four pieces the size of the nine-patch.
2. Lay the raw edges of the folded strip matching the edge of the nine-patch. Pin another strip to the opposite side.

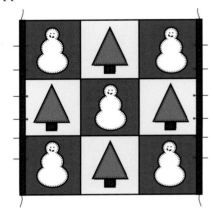

3. Repeat on top and bottom edges. Baste.
4. Do not press open. Leave folded edge loose against nine-patch.

Adding the Light Border

1. Cut two 3½" wide side borders the same length as the nine-patch measurement.
2. Pin and sew to sides. Press borders open.
3. Cut top and bottom borders the width of the nine-patch and side borders.

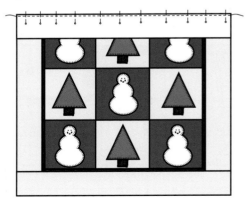

4. Pin and sew. Press open.
5. Use the 12½" Square Up ruler to trim the corners square.

Adding the Pieced Border

1. Lay out the five medium to dark border strips in a pleasing order. The end ones will lie next to each other.

2. Sew the strips together.

3. Press seam allowances in one direction. Do not leave folds at the seam lines.

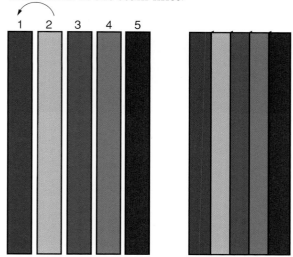

4. Cut twelve 2½" pieced strips.

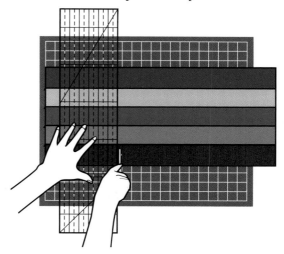

5. Sew three pieced strips together for each edge of the quilt.

6. Measure the side light borders against their pieced strips. You should be able to remove two squares from two pieced strips to fit. Measure the 13 square border against the light border.

   If it fits exactly: Pin and sew to the sides. The top and bottom 15 square strips will also fit.

If the border is too short: Trim all four sides of the light border to that measurement. Pin and sew the 13 squares to the sides. Pin and sew the 15 squares to the top and bottom.

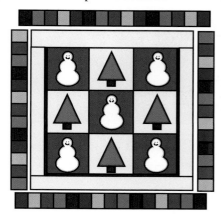

If the border is too long: Take a slightly deeper seam in several pieced border seams until pieced border fits. Repeat with top and bottom 15 square pieced borders.

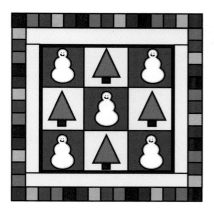

Finishing the Quilt Top

Follow the Finishing instructions on page 112.

Machine quilt in the ditch between nine-patch squares, next to folded border and between light and pieced border using invisible thread.

Embellishing the Snowmen and Trees

Hot glue or washable fabric glue embellishments if not sewn previously.

Snowman scarves: Tie knot in center and hand-sew or glue in place.

Patchwork Throughout the House

White Royal Cement Icing

2 egg whites

2 cups sifted powdered sugar

½ tsp cream of tartar

With electric mixer beat egg whites with cream of tartar until stiff. Gradually beat in 1 cup of powdered sugar. Beat 10 minutes. Add second cup of sugar and beat another 10 minutes. During last few minutes of beating add coloring if you desire. (We left ours white.) While using or storing, cover with cellophane wrap or close tightly. It sets up fast and very hard.

LuAnn Stout

We would make a candy house before Christmas, usually on Thanksgiving Day after dinner while the adults were watching the ballgame. It wasn't fancy, but it was a wonderful treat for the children, and all there participated in decorating part of the house.

A cardboard carton (soda pop cartons were just the right size) was the base, and cardboard was cut for the roof. A white royal icing was spread over the cardboard and everyone began to put on the candy. Candy canes or gum drops were used on the roof, licorice for the windows, and "m&m's" and "red hots" were doors and walks. Imaginations ran wild! Of course, we had to have a little extra candy for eating. However, the Cement Icing isn't for eating!

Nancy Loftis

Star Light! Star Bright!

*S*tar Light! Star Bright, first star I see tonight…"

Down through the ages people have watched the heavens and studied the stars. We are reminded that 2000 years ago wise men followed a star to the little town of Bethlehem.

Wallhanging size: 34" square

Materials

Dark Background
    ⅝ yd
        three 2½" wide strips
        two 10" squares

Light for Star
    ⅓ yd
        10" square

1st Medium for Four-Patches
    ¼ yd
        three 2½" wide strips

2nd Medium for Star Points
    ⅓ yd
        10" square

1st border
    ¼ yd
        four 1½" strips

2nd border, inspiration fabric
    ⅝ yd
        four 4½" wide strips

Binding
    ½ yd
        four 3" wide strips

Backing
    38" square

Batting
    38" square

Instructions

Making 20 Four-Patches

Sew ¼" seam allowance and 15 stitches to the inch or a #2 setting.

1. Assembly-line sew the Dark and 1st Medium strips together.

2. Lay closed strips on pressing mat with the Dark strip on top. Press the stitching to set the seam.

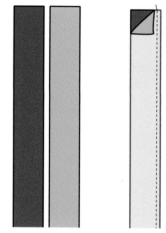

3. Lift the Dark strip and press toward the seam, pushing the seam allowance to the Dark side.

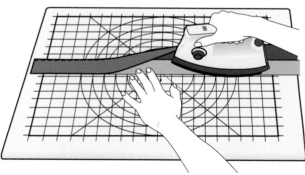

4. Place two sets of sewn strips right sides together on a cutting mat line with opposite fabrics together. Lock the seams by feeling along the seam allowance, pressing the layers to match.

5. Trim the left end straight with 6" square ruler.

6. Layer cut twenty 2½" layered pairs.

7. Assembly-line sew layered pairs.

8. Clip the threads.

9. Set seams and press seam allowance to either side.

Check several to find an average size, approximately 4½" square. Square all to your particular average measurement. This measurement will be used to square the triangle pieced squares.

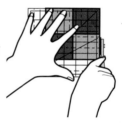

Record your four-patch measurement _____"

Making 16 Triangle Pieced Squares

1. Count out two 10" squares of Dark and one each of Light and 2nd Medium.

2. With 6" x 24" ruler and pencil, draw diagonal lines on wrong side of Light square and 2nd Medium square.

3. Place each marked square right sides together with a 10" Dark square. Pin.

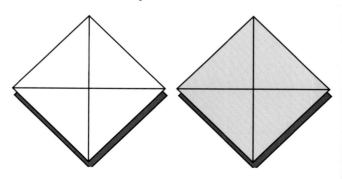

4. Assembly-line sew ¼" from diagonal line. Remove pins as you come to them.

5. Turn the chain around. Assembly-line sew ¼" from same line. Clip apart.

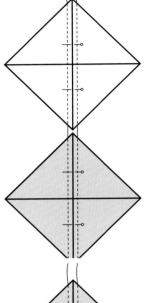

6. Repeat assembly-line sewing along both sides of the remaining diagonal lines.

7. Clip apart. Press the sewn squares.

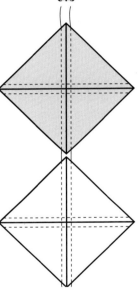

8. Rotary cut each square on both diagonal lines.

Each sewn square will make four quarters with stitching lines on two sides. Each quarter will make two pieced squares.

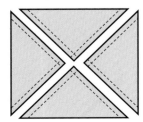 

Squaring the Blocks

Use the Quilt in a Day 6" x 12" ruler or a similar ruler marked with diagonal lines for this squaring technique. If you do not have this type of marked ruler, use any ruler and squaring technique that you are familiar with.

1. Use a 6" x 12" ruler with dashed diagonal lines at 45 degrees. Position the ruler's 4½" dashed line on the upper edge of the stitching. Center ruler along stitching between intersection and left edge.

2. Cut on both edges of the ruler.

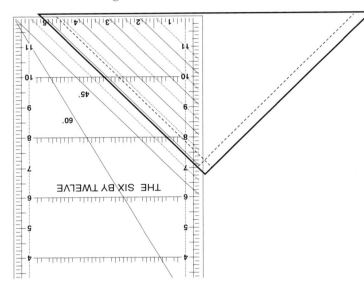

3. Open this pieced square, press and compare to the size of your four-patch measurement.

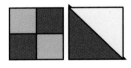

If the pieced square is larger than your four-patch, place the ruler's dashed line on or below the stitching in order to make a smaller patch.

Trim to the size of your four-patch.

4. Repeat, laying the ruler on the remaining part of that quarter and cut out another patch.

5. Trim out eight pieced squares of each combination at the size of your four-patches.

6. Trim the tips at an angle.

7. Lay a triangle on ironing board with Dark side up. Press the patch open, pushing the seam allowance to the Dark fabric.

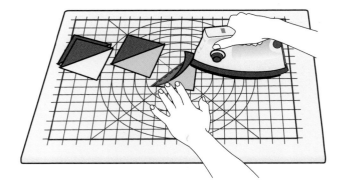

Sewing Four Blocks

1. In stacks of four lay out the nine patches that form the block. Be sure that each part is stacked consistently.

2. Flip the middle row to the left.

3. Assembly-line sew the vertical seam of rows 1 and 2.

4. Remove from machine, open and add row 3. Clip between the block sets.

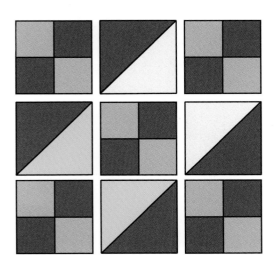

5. Sew the horizontal seams, pushing the vertical seams consistently in opposite directions away from the pieced squares.

Sewing the Four Blocks Together

1. Lay out the blocks, turning them to form the center Light star.

2. Flip the right blocks to the left.

3. Assembly-line sew the vertical seam.

4. Sew the horizontal seam pushing the vertical seam in opposite directions.

5. Press.

See Finishing instructions, page 112.

Sue Bouchard

Woven Stars

Two complementing colors of fabric are chosen so that they appear to weave back and forth to form these beautiful traditional Friendship Star patterns. To me this quilt represents how our families are brought together during the holiday season to share in the joy we bring to each other.

Color in your design.

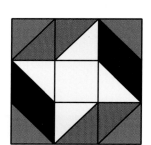

Wallhanging size: 39" square

Materials

Cut strips selvage to selvage. Avoid directional prints.

 Color one - Corners
½ yd
two 12" squares

 Color two - First ribbon
½ yd
two 12" squares

 Color three - Second ribbon
½ yd
two 12" squares

Color four - Star
½ yd
two 12" squares
3½" wide strip
nine 3½" squares

Framing border
⅓ yd
four 2" wide strips

Outside border
⅝ yd
four 4½" wide strips

Binding
⅜ yd
four 3" wide strips

Backing
1¼ yds

Hanging sleeve
⅛ yd

Batting
44" square

Instructions

Making the Pieced Squares

1. Layer and press 12" squares right sides together in these combinations with your lighter fabric on top:

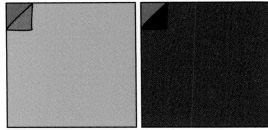

Colors 1 & 2 One of each Colors 1 & 3 One of each

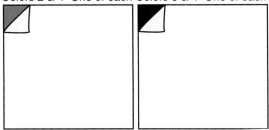

Colors 2 & 4 One of each Colors 3 & 4 One of each

2. Lay a pair of squares on the grid of the cutting mat. With a pencil and 6" x 24" ruler, draw horizontal and vertical lines 4" apart on the wrong side of the lighter fabric. Use the grid of the cutting mat.

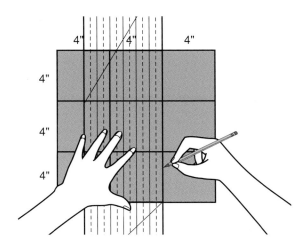

3. Draw one diagonal line across entire 12" square.

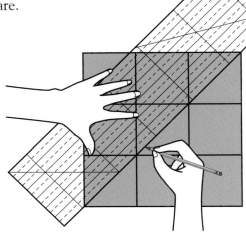

4. Draw remaining diagonal lines across the grid to form a rectangle. Each 4" square will have one diagonal line across it. Pin on each side of diagonal line in each square.

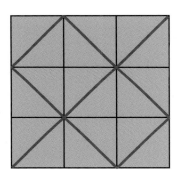

Repeat with other 12" square combinations.

5. Sew ¼" away from the one long diagonal line. Assembly-line sew remaining combinations.

6. Turn and sew ¼" from the opposite side of that line on each piece. Clip apart.

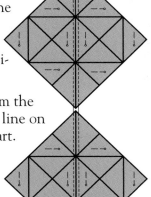

7. Continuously sew ¼" on both sides of the diagonal line forming a rectangle on all combinations.

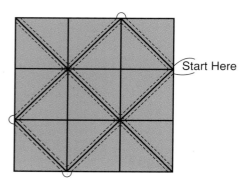

Start Here

8. Remove pins and press to set the seams.

9. Cut on horizontal, vertical and diagonal lines.

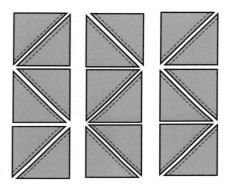

10. Lay closed triangle on pressing mat with the darker side on top. Press open, pushing the seam allowance toward the darker side.

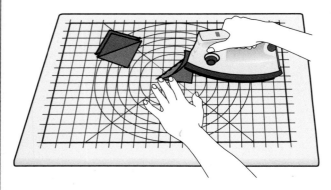

11. Square each pieced square to 3½". Center ruler's diagonal line on block's diagonal seam. Trim on two sides.

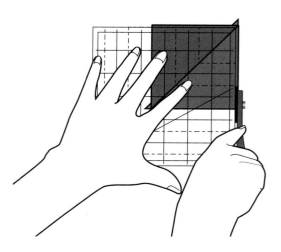

12. Line up 3½" squaring lines with newly cut edge. Trim remaining two sides.

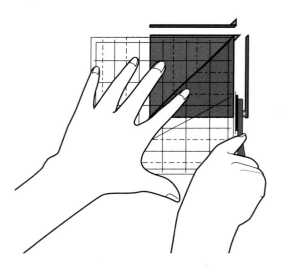

Alternate Color Placement

Explore different arrangements with two pieced squares from each color combination, plus a 3½" square of each color for the star centers. See which placement you prefer. You may want to change your mind and cut new star centers.

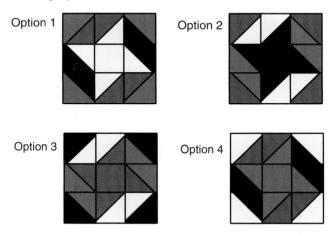

Option 1   Option 2

Option 3   Option 4

Sewing the Blocks

1. Count out and stack 9 patches in each stack.

2. Flip the middle patches to the left, right sides together. Assembly-line sew stacks.

3. Open, and assembly-line sew third row.

   Clip between blocks.

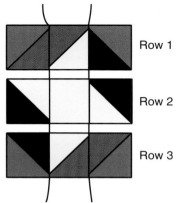

Row 1

Row 2

Row 3

4. Flip Row 1 to Row 2. Assembly-line sew, pushing top seam allowances upward and bottom seam allowances downward.

5. Open, and sew Row 3, pushing top seam allowances down and bottom seam allowances up. Press.

Sewing the Blocks Together

1. Lay out the blocks, all turned the same way.

2. Flip the middle row to the left. Assembly-line sew vertical seam.

3. Open and flip third row to second row. Assembly-line sew.

4. Sew horizontal seams.

   See Finishing instructions, page 112.

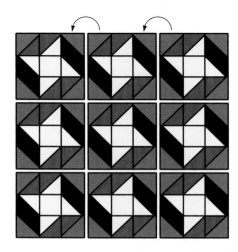

Longtime quilter, Candance L. Mittag made the beautiful two color stars Woven Star quilt pictured above.

Bachelor's Puzzle Pillow

Orion Burns

*O*ne of my many tasks at Quilt in a Day is to video tape a monthly seminar called Block of the Month. At one session the teacher and friend, Loretta Smith, challenged me to follow in my mom's foot steps. So that night, all alone in our sewing room, I went to work! The next morning I took her a finished block and illustrated instructions. That block was no longer a "Bachelor's Puzzle" to me!

Pillow size: 18" x 21"

Materials

Medium fabric in the patchwork block is also the main part of the pillow.
One way designs will need ¼ yd more fabric.
Cut strips selvage to selvage.

Medium
1 yd
    four 3½" squares
    3" x 39½" pillow side
    8½" x 39½"
    15" x 25" pillow body

Medium dark
¼ yd
    two 4" x 8"
    two 1¼" wide strips folded border

Dark
¼ yd
    two 4" x 8"
    two 1¾" wide strips block border

Light
⅛ yd
    two 4" x 8"

Other Materials
    buttons
        five ⅞" or 1" decorative buttons; can be a mixed variety of shapes and colors
    pillow
        18" square purchased form

Making own pillow form
    ⅝ yd muslin
        19½" x 39"
    batting, thick
    19" x 38" plus small scraps

Instructions

Making the Bachelor's Puzzle Patches

1. Layer 4" x 8" pieces right sides together:

   medium dark with light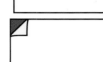

   dark with light

   medium dark with dark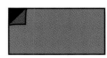

2. Draw a line at 4" on each paired rectangle.

3. Draw diagonal lines.

4. Pin. Sew ¼" from both sides of the diagonal lines.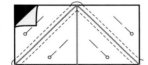

5. Press.

6. Cut apart on all lines.

7. Press seam allowances to the darker side.

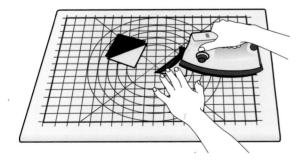

8. Square each patch to 3½" with the 6" square ruler. Center ruler's diagonal line on block's diagonal seam. Trim on two sides.

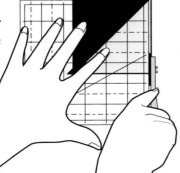

9. Turn block. Line up 3½" squaring lines with newly cut edge. Trim remaining two sides.

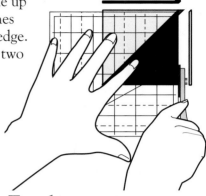

Sewing the Block Together

1. Lay out the pieces.

2. Flip Row 2 to Row 1, right sides together.

3. Assembly-line sew the vertical seam.

4. Open patches and add Row 3.

5. Open patches and add Row 4.

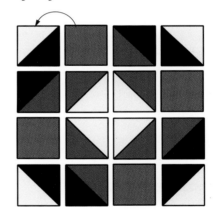

6. Sew the horizontal seams, pushing the vertical seams consistently in opposite directions.

7. Press.

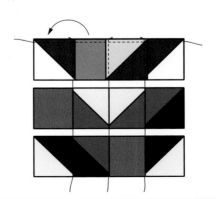

Border for Pillow Block

1. Measure sides of block and cut two 1¾" strips that measurement. Sew to block. Press open.

2. Measure top and bottom of block and cut two strips that measurement. Sew to block. Press open.

Folded Border

1. Press the 1¼" strips in half lengthwise wrong sides together.

2. Measure all four sides of the pillow block, and cut one folded border piece for each side. Pin to two sides. Do not press open.

3. Pin the remaining two border pieces. Sew. Do not press open.

    The patchwork should be approximately 15" square.

Making the Pillow Cover

1. Sew the patchwork block to the 15" x 25" piece of fabric, right sides together. Press seam. If necessary, trim strip to size of block.

2. On the long side of the 8½" x 39½" piece, fold 2" to the inside. Press. Fold again 2", and press. This forms a hem for the buttons and buttonholes.

3. Pin and sew the long strip to the patchwork strip, right sides together with folded edges on the outside. Press seams.

4. Sew the 3" wide long strip to the opposite side of the pillow cover.

5. Open out the hem that you have pressed, and pin cover together. Sew. Press the seam to one side.

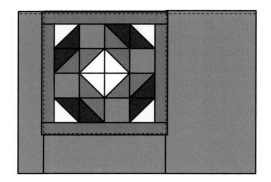

6. Re-fold the hem and stitch down.

7. Lay pillow cover flat and center patchwork. Sew opposite seam.

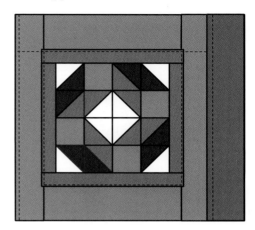

Buttons and Buttonholes

If you are really afraid to make buttonholes, you can purchase velcro to sew on the inside of the hems and sew the buttons on the front, as decoration.

1. Turn pillow cover right side out and lay flat, centering the patchwork block.

2. Measure and mark the places for your buttonholes on the top of the pillowcover. Start with the center buttonhole, and measure equally for two more buttonholes on each side of the center.

3. Make buttonholes!

4. Sew buttons to back inside of pillowcover, underneath the buttonholes.

5. Insert pillow and button up. A great gift, all finished!

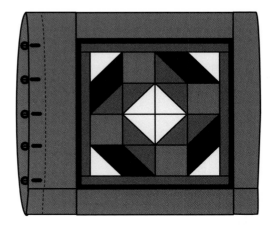

Making Your Own Pillow Form

1. For a 19" pillow, cut a piece of muslin 19½" x 39".

2. Fold and seam on two sides with ¼" seams. Turn right side out.

3. Cut a piece of scrap 16 oz. or 20 oz. batting, 19" x 38".

4. Fold in half to make square, and slide in to the muslin cover.

Fold

5. Tear or cut small bits of batting, and stuff inside the folded piece of batting. This way the pillow will not be lumpy, as all the small pieces of lumpy batting are enclosed in the smooth piece! Do not overstuff, but stuff firmly. When finished stuffing, turn the raw edges of the muslin under ¼" and stitch the pillow closed, by hand or on the machine.

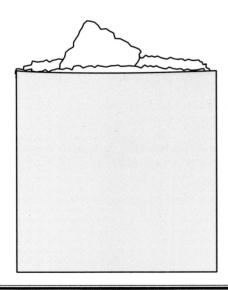

Bow Tie Wreath

*T*his four block wallhanging with blocks set on point features Christmas Wreaths made up of Bow Tie Blocks, in a new and unique way, ala "origami style." You'll never want to go back to making Bow Ties the old fashioned way after learning this neat trick, which is easy, accurate and fun, and uses the same size squares for the whole block!

Marcia Lasher

Wallhanging size: 30" square

The bow tie block is a four patch with a folded, dark square in the center. It is made from three dark squares and two light squares all the same size.

Materials
Cut strips selvage to selvage.

Background, light
⅔ yd
  13" square
  two 7" squares
  four 2½" wide strips
    (52) 2½" squares

Green fabric for wreaths & folded border
½ yd
  three 2½" wide strips
    (36) 2½" squares
  four 1½" strips

Red fabric for bows
⅛ yd
  2½" wide strip
    (12) 2½" squares

Borders & binding
¾ yd
  four 3½" wide strips
  three 3" wide strips

Backing
⅞ yd

Thin bonded batting
  32" x 32"

Instructions

Sewing the 12 Green Wreath Bow Ties

1. Stack the green wreath squares and the background squares next to your sewing machine on the left.

2. Pick up two green squares; fold one in half right side out, and lay it against the right side of the open green square with raw edges meeting on the long side.

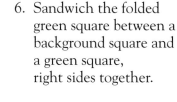

3. Lay a background square on top, right side down, matching raw edges.

4. Assembly-line sew twelve sets. Do not snip apart.

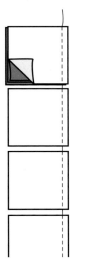

5. Flip squares to the left.

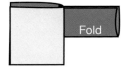

6. Sandwich the folded green square between a background square and a green square, right sides together.

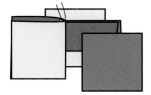

7. Assembly-line sew, enclosing the short edges of the folded square between the background and green squares. Snip apart.

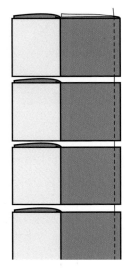

8. *Making the Origami style knot is the tricky part!* Open up the folded square from the top and refold it, lining up all raw edges and wiggle matching the center seams toward the green.

9. Pin to hold it securely in place. Stitch across carefully.

10. Open up the block and press. Voila! A wonderful three dimensional bow tie block!

Making Additional Blocks

1. Make four red blocks that will be the bows for the wreaths.

2. Make four all background fabric bow ties, for the center design in the wallhanging. Make the blocks in the same manner you made the others, disregarding the color differences.

Time Saver: Measure four sewn together wreath blocks, and cut a background square the same size approximately 8½" square.

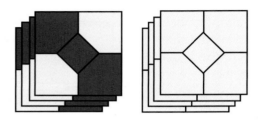

3. After all the bow tie blocks are made and pressed, "sliver trim" to approximately 4½" square.

Layout

1. Lay out the bow tie blocks in the wreath design, stacking them one on top of the other. You will have four red and green wreaths, and one all background color wreath.

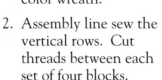

2. Assembly line sew the vertical rows. Cut threads between each set of four blocks.

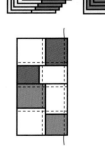

3. Open the rows, and flip over the other direction. Sew the horizontal rows. Match up the seams, flipping the seams to opposite sides to reduce the bulkiness.

4. Press when finished, in the direction that the seams lie, then turn over and press the front.

Cutting the Background Triangles

1. Cut one 13" square on both diagonals to make four triangles. These triangles are used in the top-bottom-left-right of the wreath blocks.

2. Cut two 7" squares diagonally in half to make four triangles. These triangles are used in each corner of the wallhanging, after the rest of the top is assembled.

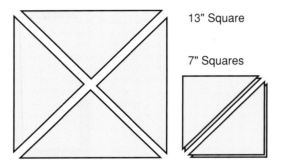

13" Square

7" Squares

Laying Out the Wreath Blocks for Sewing

1. Lay out the blocks on point. Decide if you want the bow at the top or the bottom - it's your choice!

2. Sew the rows together, making sure the square ends line up, leaving the opposite ends to hang over.

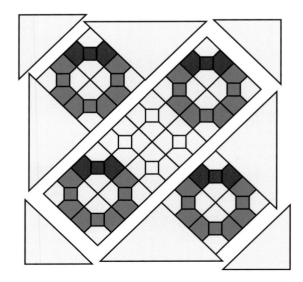

3. Lay each row of blocks back in the right order after sewing.

4. Sew these long rows together.

5. Press, making sure the seams are pressed to one side.

6. Center and pin the smaller triangles to each corner of the wallhanging. Sew.

7. Press triangles open.

8. Lay the wallhanging on the cutting mat. With the rotary cutter and ruler, trim edges even leaving ¼" seam allowance beyond the points of the block.

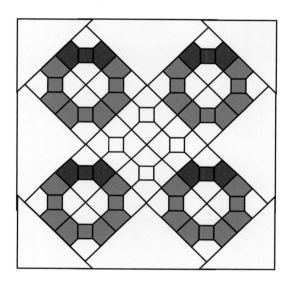

Folded Border

1. Press the two 1½" green strips in half lengthwise, wrong sides together.

2. Measure the sides of wallhanging and cut two strips this measurement.

3. Sew to wallhanging, with raw edges meeting. Do not fold out.

4. Measure top and bottom, cut two strips this measurement and sew to wallhanging as you did before. Do not fold out!

See Finishing instructions, page 112 for borders, backing, binding and casing.

Quilting

Decide how you want to quilt your wallhanging. Stitching ¼" around each of the red and green bow tie wreaths is one option. There are others. Let your imagination come up with some ideas! Rather than stitch in the ditch, trying stitching ¼" into the red border, away from the seam line. Stitch around the background bow tie knots to enhance the "origami."

Other Options

The bow tie blocks can be made other sizes by enlarging or reducing the 2½" squares that you start with.

Other ideas for using the bow tie wreath blocks include pillows or kwillows, individual wreath block wallhangings, or full-size quilts for Christmas. Try your hand at making scrap bow-tie blocks and re-arranging the design.

Scrap Bow Tie quilt made by Marilyn Erickson from 3" squares. The first border is 1¼" wide. The second border is 2" wide. The third border is 2¾" wide. Finished size is 33" x 37".

Poinsettia Wallhanging

Patricia Knoechel

*T*hese festive poinsettias can be made into pins, napkin rings, tree ornaments, or package decorations. As a variation make the flower petals in rich tones of yellow and gold to create a cheerful sunflower pin or wallhanging. Finish with brown yo yo's in the center.

Wallhanging size: 24"
Pattern provided

Materials

Centers
⅛ yd
    five 2½" circles
  or five medium to large buttons

Petals
⅓ yd
    assorted scraps of burgundys or reds and pinks
    or red color bar fabric
    cut into (34) 3¼" circles

Leaves
⅛ yd
    assorted scraps of green fabrics
    eight 4" circles

First border
⅛ yd
    two 1⅛" x 44" strips

Table
⅛ yd
    4¼" x 16"

Basket
¼ yd
    6" x 7" fabric
    6" x 7" fusible interfacing
    6" x 7" cotton batting

Background
⅜ yd
    12¼" x 16"

Poinsettia border & binding fabric
⅝ yd
    two 4" x 44" strips for border
    three 3" x 44" strips for binding

Backing & batting
    28" squares of each

Other Materials
    three 5" doilies for background
    10" doily for table scarf (cut in half)
    assortment of buttons and yo yo's (optional)
    one yd ½" ribbon for bow on basket (optional)
    low temperature glue gun

Materials for Poinsettia Pin
    nine 3¼" circles, burgundy or red
    4" circle green
    button or 2½" circle
    pin clasp
    ice cream stick
    4" doily

Instructions

Make three layered poinsettias and two smaller poinsettias with six or seven petals each.

Making the Center Yo yo's (optional)

1. Make one 2½" yo yo for each flower.

2. Thread your hand sewing needle with matching thread, double strand, and tight knot.

3. Along the outside edge, turn under ¼". Taking long stitches, sew around the outside edge.

4. Pull tight, and straighten.

5. Pull the needle through the center, and knot on back side.

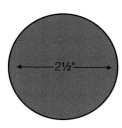

Making the Petals

1. Cut (34) 3¼" circles from burgundys or reds or color bars fabric. (An 8 oz yogurt lid is the perfect template.)

2. Stack and cut circles in half.

3. With right sides in, fold semicircles in half and assembly-line sew straight sides. Sew with 15 stitches per inch (2.0) and ¼" seam allowance.

4. Turn right sides out.

5. Center seam in back.

Fold

Making One Layered Poinsettia

1. For top layer, arrange six petals in a line. Alternate color tones, or combine all lighter tones, or all darker tones.

2. Stitch along bottom edge with a double stranded hand sewing needle. Taking long stitches, assembly-line sew from one petal to the next.

3. After stitching four petals, pull tight to gather. Continue chaining petals together and pull tight, closing center.

4. Place center yo yo or button on top to check the fit. Stitch a connecting thread and knot.

5. For bottom layer, sew eleven petals together. Leave center open.

6. Glue top layer on bottom layer.

7. Hot glue the yo yo or the button to the center.

Making the Poinsettia Leaves

1. Cut eight 4" circles.

2. Cut in half and sew as for petals.

3. Turn with seam side on bottom.

4. Turn in sides to overlap at center. Glue or hand tack.

5. Display with seam side up.

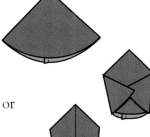

Poinsettia Pin

For Poinsettia Pin, hot glue bottom layer of eleven petals and top layer of seven petals onto 4" doily. Break ice cream stick in half and glue onto back of doily. Glue pin clasp to stick.

Making the Basket

1. Trace the basket on the smooth side of the fusible interfacing with permanent marking pen. Full size pattern included.

2. Place the dotted side of the fusible interfacing to the right side of the basket fabric.

3. Sew on the line with 20 stitches per inch. Trim seam allowance to ⅛". Cut opening in interfacing and turn right side out.

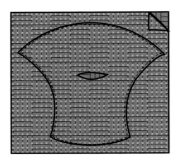

4. Cut batting to basket size and stuff inside opening.

Making the Background

1. Center and pin the half doily between the background and table fabric. Sew.

2. Press basket in place and stitch outside edge with decorative stitch or blind hem stitch with invisible thread.

3. Arrange 5" doilies on background. Sew doilies in place with 10 stitches per inch.

4. Sew or glue the flowers in place. Add optional yo yo's or buttons.

Finishing

Refer to Finishing instructions, pages 112.

Stollen

¾ cup milk scalded	2 eggs
½ cup sugar	¾ cup very soft butter
½ tsp salt	5 cups flour
2 pkgs quick dry yeast	¼ tsp nutmeg
½ cup lukewarm water	1 grated lemon rind
1 cup flour	4 cups candied fruits and nuts

Add sugar and salt to scalded milk. Cool to room temperature. Dissolve yeast in ½ cup lukewarm water. Mix with 1 cup flour and scalded milk mixture. Cover, let rise until double in bulk. Slightly beat 2 eggs and add to sponge with ¾ cup very soft butter, 5 cups sifted flour and ¼ tsp nutmeg. Also add remaining ingredients.

Turn out onto floured board and knead until very elastic or knead on floured tea towel. Add only enough flour to keep the dough from sticking. Put in a buttered bowl. Brush the top with melted butter. Cover and let rise in a warm place until double in bulk. Punch down and divide into 2 equal portions. Roll into a rectangle, ½" thick. Spread with melted butter, fold dough over lengthwise and place on lightly oiled baking sheet. Cover and let rise in a warm place until double in bulk. Bake in a moderate oven, 350 degrees, 50 minutes or if convection oven, 325 degrees for 36 minutes. When half baked, move stollen from top rack of oven to bottom rack. Dust with confectioner's sugar or confectioner's sugar icing. Store loaves overnight wrapped in plastic wrap. The flavor and texture are improved by holding. Makes 2 loaves.

Erma Knoechel

Holly Strip Pillow

Janice Orr

*T*he Holly Strip Pillow adds a festive look to couch or chair. This is a good way to use Christmas fabric scraps left from other projects. If the ruffle and holly are eliminated and youthful prints selected, it makes an easy child's project.

Pillow size: 16" square
Pattern provided

Materials

Muslin foundation
   16½" square

Lightweight batting or fleece (optional)
   16½" square

Pillow front and back
   ½ yd
      17½" square cut on diagonal
      16" square

Strips
   ⅛ yd of 5 to 8 different fabrics
      1" - 2½" wide strips

Ruffle
   ½ yd of one of the strip fabrics
      three 6" wide strips selvage to selvage

String or crochet thread
   4 yds
      four 36" long pieces

Green holly leaves
   4½" x 8" rectangle
   4½" x 8" fusible interfacing

Red holly berry
   3½" circle

16" square pillow form

Instructions

Making the Pillow Top

Cut the fabric for the stripping in varying widths to add interest to the design. Cut from 1" to 2½" wide.

1. Draw diagonal line across 16½" muslin square.

   Optional: Place muslin on top of batting or fleece and pin.

2. Right sides together, place any two strips at a right angle to the diagonal line and in the center of the triangle. Let strip extend above diagonal line about ¼".

3. Sew with ¼" seam allowance to edge of block.

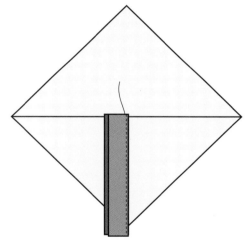

4. Open the two strips. Fingerpress strips flat.

5. Cut off excess of strips at block edge.

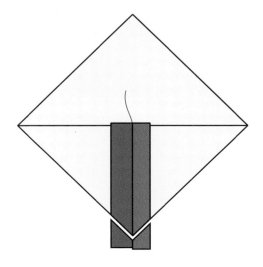

6. Continue adding strips to both sides of center strips until triangle is covered, varying width and color.

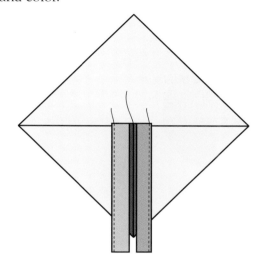

7. Trim strips from the back side. Set aside.

Making the Holly Leaves

1. Trace the holly leaf pattern onto the smooth side of fusible interfacing.

2. Place the fusible side of the traced interfacing on the right side of the green fabric. Pin.

3. Use a small stitch to machine sew on the inside edge of the line.

   Pivot at leaf points with needle in fabric. End by overlapping stitches.

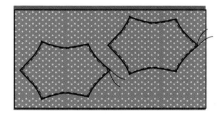

4. Trim, leaving ⅛" seam allowance. Cut a slit in the center of the interfacing and turn right side out. From the inside, use point turner/seam creaser to gently push out the curves.

Making the Holly Berry Yo yo

1. Cut a circle with a 3½" diameter from red fabric.

2. Double thread a hand sewing needle with strong thread. Knot the end. Turn under ¼" to the wrong side, and baste as you work your way around the circle. Pull tight, equalizing gathers. Push needle through center and knot.

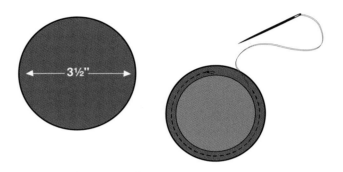

Adding the Holly Leaves and Berry

1. Place leaves in position on triangle cut from 17½" square pillow fabric. Press to fuse interfacing.

2. Stitch around leaves with either blind hem or blanket stitch.

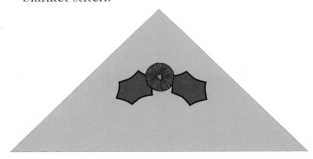

3. Attach yo yo to pillow near leaves by either bar-tacking by machine or blind hemming around outside edge.

4. Lay the triangle right sides together with the strips. Sew ¼" seam allowance from corner to corner.

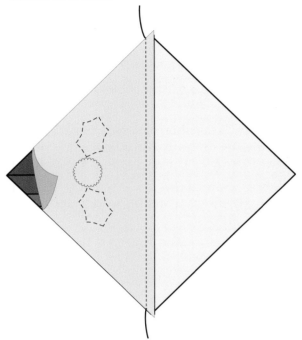

5. Fingerpress triangle open to cover muslin. Pin edges. Trim.

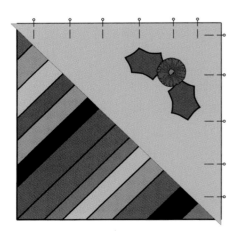

Adding the Ruffle

1. Sew three 6" wide ruffle strips end to end forming a large tube.

2. Fold in half lengthwise with wrong side together.

3. Divide strip into quarters and mark each quarter with a pen. Do not have quarter marks on any connecting seams.

4. Machine stitch a wide zigzag stitch over a string. Use a new string for each quarter.

5. Pull gathering threads so each quarter section is 16" in length.

6. Lay ruffle on right side of pillow top with string on top, matching quarter marks to corners. Pin or baste raw edges of ruffle to raw edges of pillow top equalizing gathers.

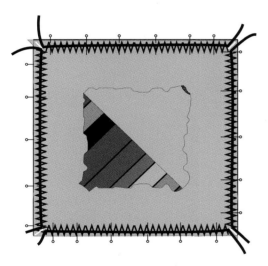

7. Lay 16" square of pillow fabric right sides together on top of ruffles and completed pillow face. Pin. Use ¼" seam allowance to sew around pillow, leaving one side open.

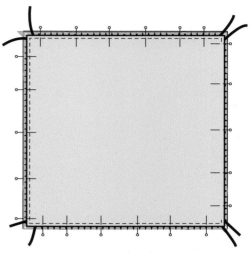

8. Turn right side out. Insert pillow form and hand stitch open side closed.

of balloons to throw later in

Grant Burn

Snowball Ba
California

Grandma's Ice Box Christmas Cookies

2 cups brown sugar

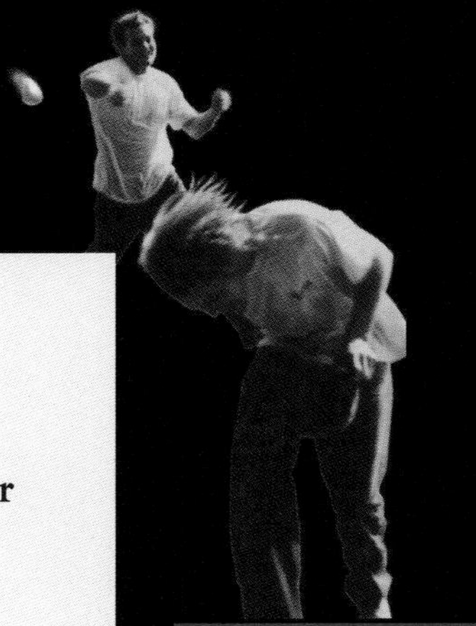

1 cup white sugar

1½ cups Crisco

3 eggs

½ cup chopped pecans

1 tsp soda dissolved in 1 tbs water

5 cups flour

Mix all ingredients together, batter will be very stiff. Make into long rolls, wrap each in wax paper. Let stand overnight in cold place. May be frozen to use later. Slice and bake in moderate oven (350 degrees) for 10-12 minutes.

Marty Halus

It wouldn't be Christmas unless these cookies were baked! My mother has moved to California, but we still make up a batch of these and send them to my brother in Indiana.

55

Star Catcher Angel

LuAnn Stout

*W*hat is more appropriate at Christmas than angels! For it was angels that first heralded the joyful news of the birth of Christ. We think of angels as protectors, watching over us and bringing us joy. This Star Catcher Angel has been designed to bring you joy all year long.

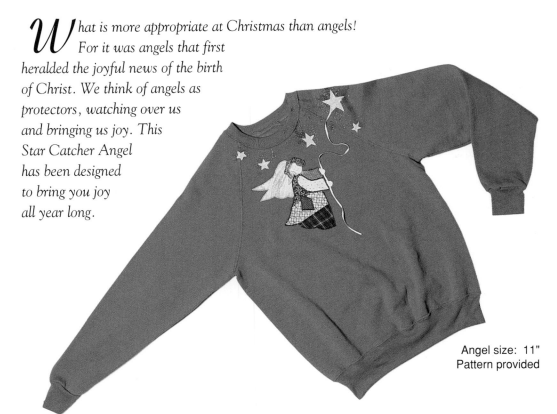

Angel size: 11"
Pattern provided

Materials

Dress
9" x 9"

Sleeve
3" x 3"

Dress patch
2½" x 2½"

Wings
6" x 5"

Face and hands
3" x 6" (may need to double face if fabric is thin)

Hair
yarn, threads from fabric
hair bow ¼" x 4½"

Star
6" x 9"

Ribbon or cord
18"

Paper backed fusible webbing
¼ yd

Tear away stabilizer
12" square

Other Materials
gold glitter fabric paint, and small stiff brush
thread to match fabrics
your choice of fabric paint colors
good quality sweatshirt

Instructions

Making the Angel

1. Place fusible paper, smooth side up, over the pattern pieces. With a pencil, trace. Trace dashed line between pieces. Cut on dashed lines.

2. Lay a protective cloth on ironing board. Place traced pattern piece on wrong side of each fabric.

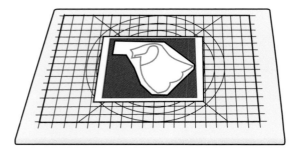

3. Lay a protective cloth over pieces, and press with hot iron about 6 seconds.

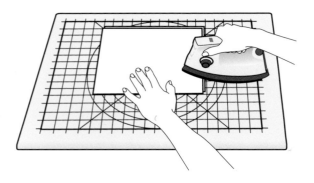

4. Cut out pattern pieces on traced lines. Peel off the paper. The fusing will stay on the fabric.

5. Place all fabric pieces on shirt in numbered order. Some pieces overlap or are placed under other pieces. Place ribbon or cord under hands and star. Carefully press pieces to the shirt about 10 seconds.

6. Place stabilizer under shirt. Finish edges with a satin stitch (tight zigzag) in matching thread, or outline with fabric paint.

7. With the permanent marking pen draw eyes and mouth onto face.

Options for the Hair

Thread hair: Ravel threads from pieces of fabric. Rub together to form a clump 3" x ½".

Yarn hair: Wrap yarn around 3" cardboard length 4 times. Tie in center. Cut loops and separate.

Shape and glue on head. Tie bow and glue in place.

Painting Stars

1. Squeeze a dab of paint onto scrap paper.

2. Dip brush tip in paint. Experiment on a scrap. Brush paint from edge of star outward. Do it lightly to look like rays from the star.

Tree Shirt

Marty Halus

This "Tree" block is easy to make and gives you the chance to use up some scraps of your fabrics. You'll want to make several to give as gifts. This is a miniature version of the beautiful tree in Wendy Gilbert's "Christmas Traditions" book. I hope that you enjoy this project as much as I did in creating it for you. Happy Holidays!

Tree size: 9½" square

Materials   Cut strips selvage to selvage.

Background
- 3" x 45" strip
    - two 1¼" x 7"
    - two 1" x 4"
    - two 2" x 3"
    - two 1½" x 3"
    - two 1½" x 4"

Tree green
- 3" x 13" strip
    - 2" x 5"
    - 1½" x 3½"
    - 1½" x 2½"

Trunk brown
- 1" x 1¼" piece

1st Border
- 1½" x 45" strip

2nd Border
- 3" x 45" strip

Other Materials

- cotton T-shirt
- ten decorative buttons

Instructions

Making the Block

Lay out the pieces according to the layout diagram.

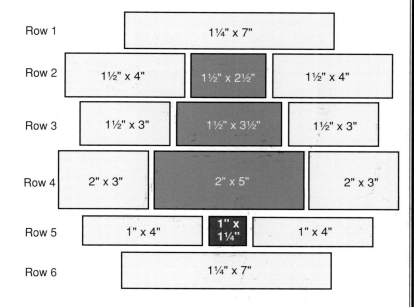

Row 1 — 1¼" x 7"

Row 2 — 1½" x 4" | 1½" x 2½" | 1½" x 4"

Row 3 — 1½" x 3" | 1½" x 3½" | 1½" x 3"

Row 4 — 2" x 3" | 2" x 5" | 2" x 3"

Row 5 — 1" x 4" | 1" x 1¼" | 1" x 4"

Row 6 — 1¼" x 7"

Sewing Row Two

1. Flip the left background piece right sides together to the tree piece. *Move the background piece in slightly while marking the diagonal. This makes the marking easier and more accurate.*

2. Draw a diagonal line on the wrong side of the fabric with a sharp pencil. Then reposition the piece before sewing. Press the two fabrics together to hold them in place.

3. Place your needle at the edge of the fabric, lined up with the pencil line. Hold the threads and sew just slightly to the outside edge of the line.

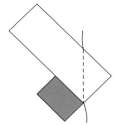

4. Add remaining background piece.

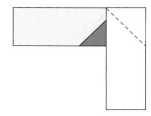

5. Trim and press seam toward tree.

Finishing the Block

1. Sew Rows 3 and 4. Use the same technique to sew both rows. Trim and press seams toward tree.

4. Square block to 5½" centering tree.

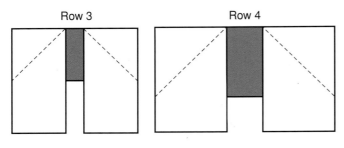

Row 3   Row 4

2. Sew Row 5, and press seams toward trunk.

3. Sew the six rows together matching the centers of each row. Press seams as shown.

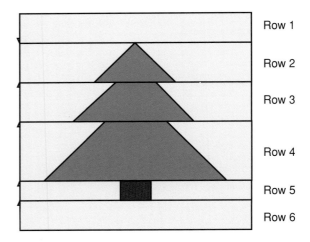

Row 1
Row 2
Row 3
Row 4
Row 5
Row 6

Adding the First Border

1. Cut 2 strips 1½" x 5½" (or the size of your block).

2. Pin and sew to sides of block.

3. Press open.

4. Cut 2 strips 1½" by the opened width of your block, approximately 7½".

5. Pin and sew to the top and bottom of the block.

6. Press open.

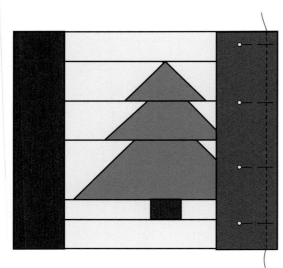

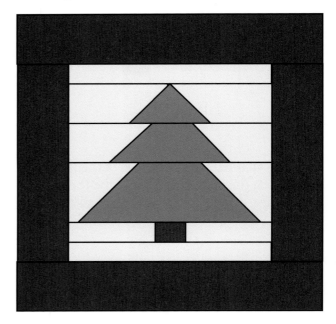

Adding the Second Border

1. Fold 3" wide strip in half wrong sides together. Press.

2. Cut two side pieces the height of your block, approximately 7½".

3. Match the raw edges. Pin.

4. Sew the side borders. Press open.

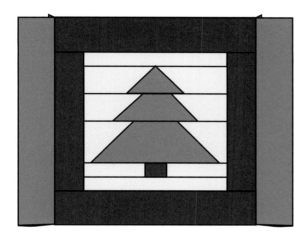

5. Cut two pieces the width of the block plus ½", approximately 10".

6. Tuck in about ¼" on both ends to fit the width of the block. The fold will be the outside edge of the block.

7. Pin and sew top and bottom borders to block.

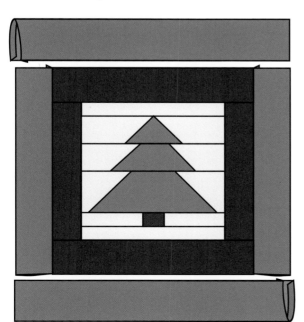

8. Press borders open.

Sewing the Block to the Shirt

1. Carefully position block on shirt. Measure equal distance from arms, and down from neckline to block corners. Pin.

2. Use invisible or other thread. Sew a zigzag or decorative stitch around the outside edge.

3. Stitch in the ditch between borders and between border and edge of block.

Embellishing the Sleeves

1. Turn up sleeves twice in 1" folds.

2. Sew on five decorative or plain buttons spaced evenly around each folded sleeve.

Yo yo Tree and Wreath

Eleanor Burns

Simply made yo yo's in shades of green form a Christmas tree or wreath easily sewn to any garment for a festive touch. Then let your creative spirit decorate it!

This is a perfect "holiday travel" project. Cut stacks of circles before your trip, make yo yo's while enroute, and sew them to the base upon your arrival.

Adult tree size: 11"
Child tree size: 8"

Adult wreath size: 8½"
Child wreath size: 6½"

Materials

Greens
　　five ⅛ yd each

Brown (tree only)
　　⅛ yd

Sweatshirt, jumper or other garment

Other Materials (optional)

Tree only
　　7½" doily for tree skirt
　　1" star button for top
　　narrow gold rick-rack

Tree or Wreath
　　½" red buttons
　　gold beads
　　jumper: four ⅝" star buttons

Instructions

Making the Yo yo's

1. Layer cut 3" circles from the green fabric.

Tree	Adult: 42	Wreath	Adult: 32
	Child: 28		Child: 25
Trunk	Brown: 2		

2. Double thread a hand sewing needle with strong thread. Knot the end. Turn under ¼" to the wrong side, and baste around the circle. Pull tight, equalizing gathers. Push needle to the back side and knot.

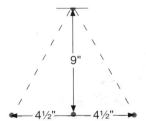

Making Yo yo Tree or Wreath

1. Slip a square ruler between layers of shirt or jumper.

2. Find the center and mark the placement of the design.

Adult Tree: Measure and mark at 9". Mark 4½" in both directions. Connect lines for triangle shape.

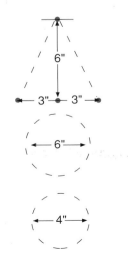

Child Tree: Measure and mark at 6". Mark 3" in both directions. Connect lines for triangle shape.

Adult Wreath: Draw on a 6" circle with chalk.

Child Wreath: Draw on a 4" circle with chalk.

3. Place yo yo's randomly by color to form shapes and pin in place.

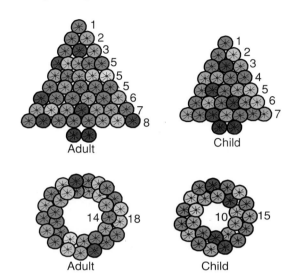

Adult   Child

Adult   Child

Hand Sewing Yo yo's to Base

Hand sew with a curved needle. Use a long running stitch, catching each yo yo several times.

Machine Sewing Yo yo's to Base

Thread your machine with invisible thread on the top, and match bobbin thread to base. Set your machine with the stitch for sewing on buttons.

Catch both sides of the yo yo as you continuously sew across the rows. Clip all threads when you are finished.

Optional Embellishments

Tree

Fold the doily in half, and hand stitch in place for a tree skirt.

Sew on narrow rick-rack.

Tree and Wreath

Sew the red buttons through all thicknesses.

Sew small gold beads to centers of yo yo's.

Mantel Decorations

This poem was passed down from my grandmother, Emma Riggs Chinn, of Flatwoods, KY, to my father Lloyd Chinn, who passed it down to me to pass on to my children, Sarajane, Paul and Valerie. I have always enjoyed it and hope you will, too.

"T'was the Night after Christmas"

T'was the night after Christmas, the fires were all out;
And silence reigned, within and without.
When suddenly was heard a shriek, loud and shrill,
From the children's bedroom, which before was so still.

The father jumped out of his bed in a fright,
And hastily seizing a match, struck a light!
He rushed to the bedroom filled with children so dear;
And mother was following, her heart filled with fear.
They opened the door and were greeted with cries

And groans from the children with tears in their eyes.
"Oh! Mama, how my stomach does ache!
I think I've eaten too much cake,
And turkey, jelly, and mince pie.
Do hurry for the doctor or I surely will die!"

The doctor soon came with saddle bags full
Of syrup, and powders, and boxes of pills.
He worked all night and part of the next day.
Presented the bill and then went away.

The father looked at the bill and did grumble and splutter,
While his good wife flew around in a comical flutter.
She said as she looked at her children so dear,
"Well, I'm glad that Christmas comes just once a year."

Author Unknown – submitted by Nancy Loftis

Courthouse Steps Stockings

Judy Knoechel

*C*hristmas stockings are my favorite symbol of Christmas and Courthouse Steps is my favorite quilt pattern. This winning combination is a quick and easy sewing project, perfect to grace your mantel and give to friends.

Stocking: 18"
Pattern provided

Materials

Cut strips selvage to selvage.

Center, medium
⅛ yd
    1½" wide strip

Color A, light strips
¼ yd
    four 1½" wide strips

Color B, dark strips
¼ yd
    four 1½" wide strips

Batting
16" x 21"

Lining, muslin
½ yd

Backing
½ yd

Cuff
⅓ yd
    8" x 20"

Ribbon
6"

Pattern tracing paper
15" x 19"

Instructions

Arranging the Fabric Strips

Arrange folded strips in the following order to the right of the sewing machine.

Center

A Color

B Color

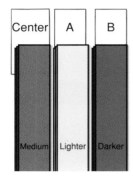

Making the Blocks

Use ¼" seam allowance and 12-15 stitches per inch or #2 on machine settings with 1-4.

1. Unfold one strip of each: Center, A strip, B strip.

2. Stack on cutting mat. Cut at 20".

Sewing the Center

Use 20" strips.

1. Put A right sides together with Center. Sew the length of the strip.

2. Lay on the ironing board with A on top. Lightly press to set the seam.

   Lift the upper strip and press toward the fold. The seam will fall behind the strip on top. Make sure there are no folds at the seam line.

   Turn strip over and check that the seam is pressed in the right direction.

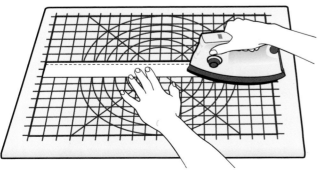

3. Sew B to opposite side of Center.

4. Lay sewn strips on ironing board with B on top.

   Set the seam and press open.

5. Lay sewn strips on gridded cutting mat, lining bottom edge with grid line. Square left side.

   Cut ten 1½" blocks.

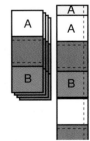

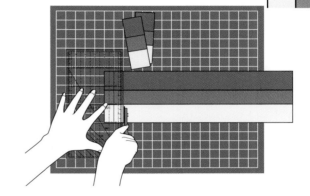

Adding the Second A and B

Stack going in the same direction.

1. Lay blocks right side down in this order:

2. Lay A strip right side up under presser foot. Sew blocks to strip.

3. Lay strip on cutting mat with block side on top. Lay the ruler's horizontal line on top edge of block and the right edge of ruler along side of block. Cut. Repeat.

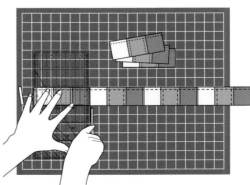

4. Lay blocks on ironing mat with A on top. Set the seam and press open. Stack in same direction.

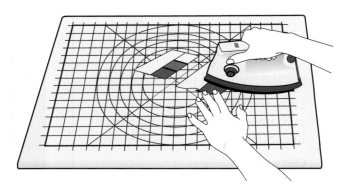

5. Lay blocks right side down with A on left. Sew blocks to B strip.

6. Cut apart and stack in same direction.

7. Lay blocks on ironing mat with B on top. Set seam and press open.

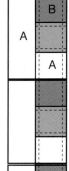

Adding the Third A and B

1. Lay blocks right side down in this order:

2. Sew to A strip.

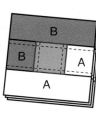

3. Flip strip so the last block becomes the first block and the A strip is on the left. Lay out a B strip.

4. Sew blocks to B strip.

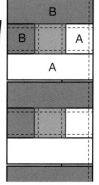

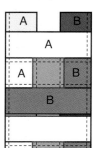

5. Cut apart.

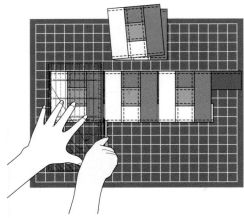

6. Lay closed block on ironing mat with strips on top. Open and press both A and B.

Adding the Fourth A and B

1. Lay blocks right side down in this order:

2. Lay A strip under presser foot. Add all blocks.

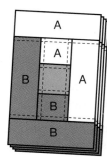

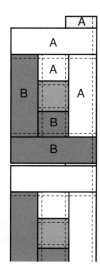

3. Flip blocks so A strip is on left. Add B strip.

4. Repeat cutting and pressing steps.

5. The blocks are now complete.

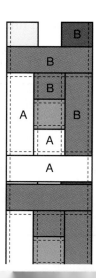

Sewing the Blocks Together

1. Arrange your blocks in stocking shape layout.

2. Sew together.

3. Press.

Quilting the Stocking Together

1. Lay out batting. Center patchwork stocking on top of batting.

2. Pin pattern to right side of patchwork.

3. Cut out with scissors or rotary cutter.

4. Remove pattern. Pin.

5. "Stairstep" machine quilt or stitch around blocks.

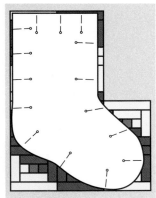

Completing the Stocking

1. Lay out one backing piece wrong side up.

2. Lay muslin lining, (or printed muslin) folded in half, right sides together, on top of backing.

3. Lay paper stocking pattern on top. Pin.

4. Cut with scissors or rotary cutter.

Single layer backing, right side down

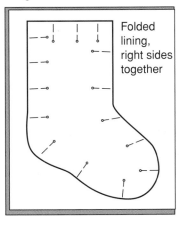

Folded lining, right sides together

5. Lay out quilted stocking, right side up. Lay the stocking back right side down on patchwork.

6. Lay both stockings cut from lining on top. Pin.

7. Stitch around the outside edge with a generous ¼" seam allowance. Leave top open. Clip at curves.

8. Reach between back of stocking and patchwork. Turn right side out. Check that all layers were sewn.

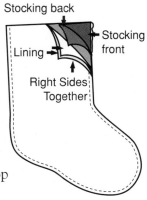

Stocking back

Stocking front

Lining

Right Sides Together

Adding the Cuff

1. Measure around the opening of the stocking top. Record measurement. Add ½"= length of strip.

2. Cut 8" strip at that length.

3. Fold the strip in half, right sides together. Sew the ends together. Press seam allowance open.

4. Turn right side out. Fold in half the other way to form a circle. The seam allowance is on the inside.

5. Pull two lining pieces apart. With the raw edges up and seam to the left, tuck the cuff inside the stocking between linings. Match the cuff seam with the stocking seam. Place one pin at the matched seam.

6. Loop the 6" of ribbon. Tuck loop between cuff and stocking to the right of the matched seam. Leave ends showing. Pin remaining edges.

7. Sew with a ¼" seam allowance around top.

8. Pull cuff out and fold down.

Stitch

Holiday Stockings

Nancy Loftis

Stockings hung on the mantel evoke strong feelings of a warm cozy home, anticipation of family together, a time for renewal and putting differences behind us – each stocking somehow representing its owner's presence in our heart as well as in our home.

Stocking size: 18"
Patterns provided

Materials

Beary Christmas

Bear should be a "tone on tone" or textured fabric.

Bear body, head, ears
8½" x 11" dark brown

Bear face, paws, inner ear
4¼" x 8½" medium or light brown

Bow tie & gift bow
4" x 7" medium red
2" x 2½" medium red

Package
5" square green plaid or small print

Package ribbon
1" x 10" medium red cut on bias

Lightweight fusible interfacing
11" x 17"

Stocking
½ yd beige

Lining
½ yd muslin

Cuff
8" x 20" green plaid or small print

Loop
6" ribbon or 3½" x 8" green plaid or small print

Batting
16" x 21"

Cotton batting (optional)
7" square for stuffing bear face, paws and package

Other Materials

Mouth, outline of package
black embroidery floss, embroidery needle

Eyes, nose
purchased button eyes & nose

Gilded Poinsettia

Leaves
3½" x 10" dark green
6" x 7½" medium green

Petals
7½" x 8½" bright red
5" x 11" dark red
4"x 10" light red

Lightweight fusible interfacing
11" x 17"
6" x 7½"

Stocking
½ yd white or off-white

Lining
½ yd muslin

Cuff
8" x 20" dark red

Loop
6" ribbon or 3½" x 8" dark green

Batting
16" x 21"

Other Materials

Centers of poinsettias
yellow embroidery floss, embroidery needle

Veins of petals & leaves (optional)
gold metallic thread

plastic drinking straw

ballpoint bodkin

point turner and seam creaser or "wooden iron"

15" x 19" pattern tracing paper

Instructions

General Applique Instructions for Gilded Poinsettia and Beary Christmas Stockings

1. Remove the pattern sheet from the book and unfold.

2. Place 11" x 17" piece of fusible interfacing smooth side up on the pattern sheet. Trace all pieces with a fine, permanent pen. Include the dashed lines. Repeat for the four large size medium green leaves on the 6½" x 7½" piece of fusible interfacing.

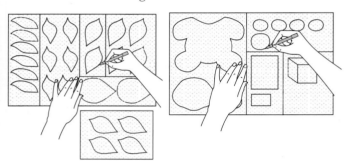

3. Cut interfacing apart on long dashed lines. Place each interfacing piece on each corresponding fabric piece with the textured "dotted" side against the right side of fabric. The smooth side of interfacing is on top. Pin in the center of each pattern piece. **Do not press.**

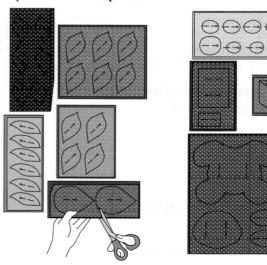

4. Sew on the inside edge of the line with a small stitch (20 stitches per inch).

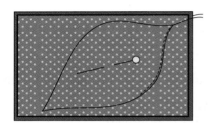

5. Trim each piece to ⅛" from the line around the outside edge. Clip at corners. Cut a small slit in interfacing for turning.

6. Turn with a ball point bodkin and a plastic straw. *Insert straw into slit in interfacing. With the end of the straw on the fabric, gently push the fabric into the straw with the ball point end of the bodkin. Push smaller pieces with bodkin through straw, turning the piece at the same time. Pull larger pieces off straw and turn.*

   Turn leaves one end at a time.

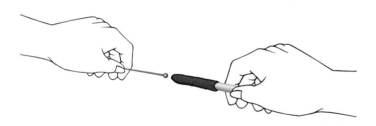

7. Crease fabric edges with seam creaser or wooden iron.

8. (Optional) Stuff bear's face, paws, and package with cotton batting for more dimension.

9. Position pieces on the stocking referring to the photograph on page 70. (Save bear tie and package for later.) Place a pressing cloth over stocking to prevent possible scorching and dirt from the iron. Using cotton setting and steam, firmly press pieces to stocking. Once fused, press from back side.

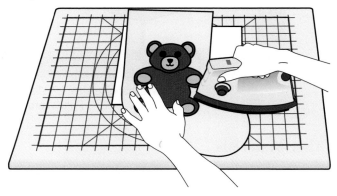

10. Finish the applique design by machine edge stitching with a straight stitch, or invisible thread and a blind hem stitch for a hand appliqued look. The designs can also be appliqued by hand. Stitch, following the design.

Poinsettia: With yellow embroidery floss, make French knots in the centers of the flowers. Hand outline stitch veins on the leaves and petals with gold metallic thread.

Beary Christmas: **For Bow Tie,** fold the 2" x 2½" piece of medium red fabric in thirds lengthwise, then loop around the bow. Stitch loop in back. Press bow in place.

For Face, outline the mouth with a stem stitch using black embroidery floss and an embroidery needle. Sew on the button nose and eyes.

Additional outline quilting may be done for added dimension.

For Package, add dimension with additional stem stitching to outline the box. Fold 1" x 10" medium red bias into thirds lengthwise. Wrap around package, trim to size. Tuck ends under package and press package in place. Stitch. Hand stitch ribbon in place. Loop remaining bias strip around gift bow, trim to size. Stitch loop in back. Press bow in place. Stitch.

Completing Stocking

Complete stocking according to illustration and instructions on page 69.

Stained Glass Wreath

Luckie Yasukochi

*T*his wallquilt showcases the three crafts I dearly love: quilting, applique, and working with stained glass. You, too, can create a quilted window in which appliqued pieces are substituted for colored glass, and a satin stitch for lead seams. The effects are strikingly similar. I hope you have as much fun with this wall-hanging as I did planning and making it!

Wallhanging size: 27½" square
Pattern provided

Materials

Cut strips selvage to selvage.

Background, light
⅔ yd
24" square

Bow
4½" x 8"

Bells
7" x 10½"

Bell ringer
2½" x 2½"

Wreath
⅓ yd

Window pane, frame and binding
⅞ yd
1½" wide strip, pane
four 3" wide strips, frame
four 3" wide strips, binding

Backing
1 yd

Batting
1 yd

Paper backed fusible webbing
1 yd

Tear away stabilizer
⅞ yd

Other Materials

sewing machine that makes a satin stitch (tight zigzag)

new needle, size 12 or embroidery needle

thread, color of your frame

fusible thread

large spool black thread

permanent marker, fine to medium point

marking pencils for both light and dark fabric

Optional

⅜" bias bar

6 mm wide twin needle

applique foot or one with a groove on the bottom

Light box
or method of tracing lines of pattern pieces onto fabric. Place paper backed fusible webbing against wrong side of fabric.

Instructions

Tracing Placement Pattern onto Background

1. Place Placement Pattern right side up on table. Center the 24" background square right side up on pattern. If lines don't show through fabric, use a light box (or your substitute).

2. With a soft lead pencil, lightly draw enough of the pattern to show where to place.

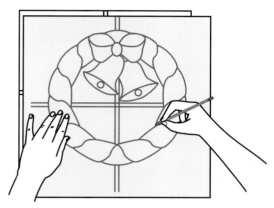

Drawing Pattern Pieces

1. Lay Pattern Piece sheet on table.

2. Place paper backed fusible webbing on top, paper side up.

3. With permanent marker, trace all pattern shapes and lines.

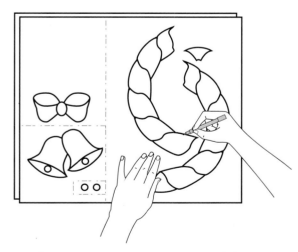

Notice the pattern is a mirror image of the finished design.

4. Cut patterns on dashed lines to separate shapes. Do not remove paper side.

Fusing Patterns to Fabric

1. Pair each pattern shape with its fabric.

2. Place fabric wrong side up on pressing mat. Lay fusible side against wrong side of fabric.

3. Use a hot, dry iron on cotton setting. Press all areas about 3 seconds.

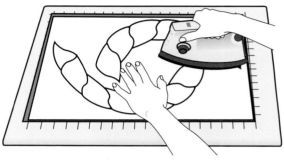

4. Cut out each shape on outside line. Do not remove paper.

5. Using a light box (or your substitute), place paper side against light. Draw lines for satin stitching onto right side of fabric.

Making the Window Panes

1. Fold (do not press) 1½" wide pane strip in half lengthwise, wrong sides together.

2. Use fusible thread in the bobbin. Sew ¼" seam allowance.

3. Center the seam on one side. (If using ⅜" bias bar, insert in tube and push seam to center of one side. Press.) Push seam to expose fusible thread. Trim seam.

4. Cut pieces to fit lengths indicated on Placement sheet.

5. Lay pieces on marked background. See photo for placement. The Bell and Wreath pieces will overlap this frame.

6. Press with hot, dry iron to hold pane in place for sewing.

7. Topstitch in place with matching thread, either a 6 mm twin needle or by stitching on both edges.

Appliqueing the Pieces

1. Cut out each fused pattern piece on outside of traced lines.

2. Remove paper from fused and marked pieces.

3. Place Wreath pieces, Bells piece and Bow on background.

4. When satisfied, use hot, dry iron to fuse pieces in place.

Satin Stitching Practice on a Test Piece

1. Layer tear away stabilizer on piece of scrap material.

2. Use an applique foot or foot with groove on bottom.

3. Use black thread both in top and bobbin.

4. Use a new needle in your machine, size 12. Set stitch length (about 0.4) and stitch width (about 3.0). It should be close enough so that it looks like a solid line.

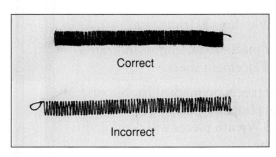

5. Refer to owner's manual to make a zigzag or satin stitch.

6. Experiment sewing until you have satisfactory satin stitch.

Satin Stitching

1. Place background fabric on tear away stabilizer. Pin in place.

2. Satin stitch Wreath lines in order given:

Steps One and Two

Satin stitch should cover the applique piece and barely catch the background.

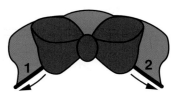

Step Three

Start from outside edge of three and stitch to end.

Step Four

Start by Step Three and stitch to the end.

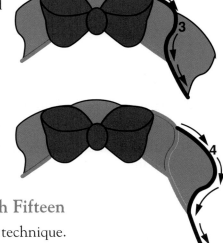

Steps Five through Fifteen

Repeat stitching technique.

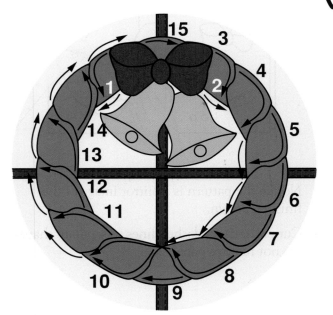

3. Stitch inside Bell lines and Bell ringers.

    For circles, take just a few stitches and then pivot by lifting up your presser foot and leaving your needle in down position outside of your circle.

4. Stitch outside Bell lines in order given.

    To do a point, stitch 2 or 3 stitches past the point with needle in down position on the outside of point, turn and stitch up the other side of point.

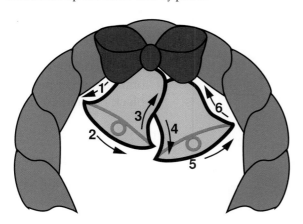

5. Stitch inside lines of Bow.

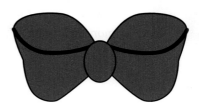

6. Then stitch outside lines.

    Satin stitch should cover the raw edges where bow meets wreath and bells.

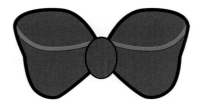

7. Stitch circle last.

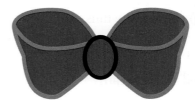

    Add frame border.

    See Finishing instructions, page 112.

Machine Quilting

1. Use thread to match background on top, and thread to match the backing in the bobbin.

2. Use a larger stitch, about 10 to the inch. Outline stitch near pieces.

3. Stitch around both sides of window pane, around the Wreath inside and outside, around the Bells, and "in the ditch" around the frame.

Anne Dease

Bountiful Wreath

What would be more pleasant at Christmas time than a holiday wreath on your front door? This wreath uses a variety of nuts, fruits and cinnamon sticks with a friendly snowman to welcome your guests for the season.

Materials

Wreath

Wire edge craft ribbon
- 2½" x 3 yds
  - 7" piece for loop
  - 20" piece for top bow
  - 28" piece for lower bow
  - 53" piece for bow tails

24" Purchased green wreath

pine cones

nuts

two apples

two oranges

eight cinnamon sticks

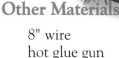

Other Materials
8" wire
hot glue gun

6" Snowman

100% Cotton batting
- two 5" x 7"

Scarf
- 2" x 6"

Face
- round toothpick
- orange marker pen
- black permanent marker

Other Materials
- small twigs for arms
- three buttons for snowman front
- black thread for blanket stitch
- polyester stuffing

Instructions

Wreath size: 26"
Pattern provided

Drying the Fruit

Dehydrate the apples and oranges by slicing into ¼" inch slices. Heat oven to 250 degrees, then turn heat off. Set fruit slices on tray and let dry slowly. If you have a gas oven, the pilot light will be enough to keep the oven temperature at a good temperature for drying. If you have an electric oven, you may need to reheat the oven after a few hours, then turn it off again to maintain a degree of heat until the dehydrating is complete. This usually takes 48 hours.

Making the Wreath

1. Make a hanger from 8" of wire on the back of the wreath. Hang while you are decorating it.

2. Using a hot glue gun, place dehydrated fruits, cones and cinnamon sticks in desired patterns.

3. Make large bow, and place streamers of ribbons through the wreath.
   Bow: Make two loops with the 20" and 28" pieces. Layer on center of streamer piece. Wrap with 7" loop piece and twist in back.

4. Glue snowman at the bottom of the wreath.

Making the Snowman

1. Cut out Snowman pattern and lay on top of two layers of batting. Carefully cut around pattern. Blanket stitch around snowman, leaving an opening at the bottom. Gently stuff, making sure not to stuff him to tightly. Blanket stitch the opening shut.

2. Draw a face on snowman with permanent marker.

3. Color the tip of a toothpick with an orange marker. Break off a length long enough for snowman's nose.

4. Knot scarf on snowman.

5. Glue buttons, nose and scarf to snowman. Glue twigs to the sides of the snowman, between the blanket stitches.

Cinnamon Broom Dolly

Teresa Varnes

Doll size: 17"

I love to make beautiful dresses for my two young daughters, Melissa and Amber. These Cinnamon Broom Dolls remind me of them. The doll is easy to make because her skirt and sleeves are just edged rectangles of fabric fixed to a cinnamon or other flavored craft broom. Add contrasting bow sash, curls, and a straw hat with flower for a scented decoration. Scraps from girls' clothing are perfect!

Materials

Dress
¼ yd
- 9" x 20" skirt
- 5" x 8" sleeves
- 1½" x 10" or length to fit your hat choice for hat band
- 2" x 3" bow's knot

Sash
¼ yd
- two 2½" x 9" bow tails
- 2½" x 18" lower bow
- 2½" x 14" upper bow

Lace
1 yd
- 1¼" - 1½" wide for skirt and sleeves

Other Materials
- dolly curly hair one package
- straw hat, 6" across
- ⅛" ribbon 25" long for skirt's drawstring
- craft broom, cinnamon or other spice 12" tall
- ribbon rose
- hot glue gun

Instructions

Making Skirt and Sleeves

Double fold, press and sew ¼" hem on sides of dress and four sides of sleeve. Sew lace to one 20" skirt side and both 5" sleeve sides.

Skirt: Fold and press ¼" hem on remaining 20" side. Fold ½" more to provide casing for the ⅛" wide ribbon drawstring. Sew. Feed ribbon through casing with safety pin or bodkin. Put skirt around broom handle and gather with drawstring. Tie skirt to broom.

Sleeves: Fold and press in half to find center. Sew a long gathering stitch on center fold. Gather and glue midway down broom handle, leaving a gap between sleeves and skirt.

Making the Layered Bow

1. Fold and press only a ¼" hem on 9" sides of both tails. Zigzag hems with matching thread.

2. Fold in half lengthwise, and cut end on an angle.

3. Gather the square ends of the tails into thirds. Overlap them ¼" and sew. Glue to top of skirt.

4. Fold and press only a ¼" hem on long sides of 2½" x 18" bow piece. Zigzag hems with matching thread.

5. Fold and press in half to find center. Fold one end ½" beyond center. Fold the other end ½" beyond center.

6. Repeat with 2½" x 14" bow piece.

7. Fold 2" x 3" skirt fabric rectangle in thirds for knot on bow.

8. Layer smaller bow on top of larger bow. Sew on center line and pinch. Glue knot band around the bow.

9. Glue bow on top of bow tails at top of skirt.

Making the Hat Band

1. Fold in edges ½" on long sides of 1½" x 10" piece. Lightly glue to hold folds in place.

2. Glue hat band to crown. The ends should meet, not overlap. Glue on flower or decoration.

Finishing

1. Glue layers of curly hair to backside of hat under the flower or decoration.

2. Place glue on bow. Position hat so that the hair is glued to the bow.

3. Glue the top of the sleeves to sides of hat to stabilize.

Gingerbread Cookies

5 cups flour

4 tsp cinnamon

2¼ tsp baking soda

1 tsp ground cloves

2 cups dark molasses

⅓ cup water

1 tsp salt

2 tsp ginger

1 cup butter

3 eggs

Cream butter till light. Beat in molasses, then eggs. Blend in water. Stir dry ingredients together, then stir into butter mixture. Chill at least 1 hour. Roll dough to ¼" thickness on lightly floured surface. Cut into desired shapes. If hanging as an ornament, poke hole at top with stiletto. If decorating with raisins, add before baking. Place on ungreased cookie sheet. Bake at 350 degrees, 15 minutes for eating or 18 to 20 minutes for an ornament.

Eleanor Burns

decorates a half dozen different trees every year. Each small tree in a separate room has a different theme, such as all Santas or all angels. It is wonderful to visit her home and have a tour. She explains the various ornaments and where they came from. You can make this a tradition for yourself or family members, adding a particular type of ornament to each collection.

Penny Major

About two weeks before Christmas we made sugar cookies. They were rolled, cut into all different Christmas designs, baked, cooled, frosted and decorated. The cookies were then tied on the small Christmas tree in the family room as ornaments. Whenever friends or playmates came, they could choose and eat a cookie from the tree. Needless to say, lots of friends stopped by for cookies!

Sour Cream Sugar Cookies

1½ cups sugar

1¼ cups butter

1 tsp vanilla

2 eggs

¾ tsp soda

2 tsp baking powder

3½ cups flour

½ tsp nutmeg

1 cup sour cream

Cream sugar and butter well. Add eggs and vanilla. Sift dry ingredients together and add, alternating with sour cream. Chill dough several hours or overnight. It will be very soft and must be chilled to handle. Roll out on lightly floured board into desired shapes and bake.

LuAnn Stout

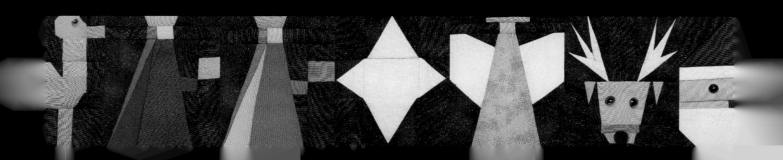

Decorating the Tree

Angel Ornament

Patricia Knoechel

I have been collecting angels for years, and I enjoy giving Angels as gifts. With each angel gift, I attach a note which reads "Hang this angel on your tree to remind you that God has placed a real angel in Heaven who's watching over you."

Angel size: 7"

Materials

White fabric strip for sleeves
2½" x 10"

All Battenburg doily for wings
6"

Battenburg doily with fabric center for dress
6"

Narrow ribbon
12"

Other Materials

doll hair (Mini curl)

5" gold star garland or 4" plastic string pearls

hand held decorations as ribbon flowers, candle, halo, small ornament, gift package, bell, star, or musical instrument

1" ball knob "doll head" with one flat side

ice cream stick

5" pipe cleaner

12" gold cord for hanging

low temperature glue gun

bodkin

Instructions

Wings

1. Remove labels from doilies. Fold All Battenburg doily in half right side out.

2. Take tuck in center. Hot glue tuck and cool.

3. Cut ice cream stick in half and glue on center top of wings, with 1" neck extending above wings.

4. Glue head to top of ice cream stick with flat side down.

Sleeves

1. Fold 2½" x 10" strip in half to measure 1¼" x 10".

2. Mark and sew, leaving 1" open in center.

3. Trim and turn right side out over straw with bodkin or chopstick. Trim off ⅛" at points.

4. Insert pipe cleaner through center opening. To make "hands," push ends of pipe cleaners through pointed ends. Push back sleeve and twist hands together. Push sleeves over exposed pipe cleaner and glue together.

5. Glue center opening shut.

6. Glue sleeves to ice cream stick, right below head.

Dress

1. With doily right side up and pattern centered, fold top over 1".

2. Tuck sides in to center. Balance sides evenly. Hand press pleats. Glue down pleats at top.

3. Glue dress right below sleeves.

Embellishments

1. For hanging, knot together ends of gold cord and glue to top of head.

2. Cut mini doll hair into 1" lengths. Working in small sections, apply hot glue to doll head. Place hair in hot glue quickly before it cools.

3. To make halo, twist together ends of star garland to form a circle. If using pearls, glue ends together to form circle. Slip halo over hanging cord to fit onto head.

4. Embellish hands with flower and bow, or other decoration.

Sue Bouchard & Sue Sells

Following Yonder Star

*D*reaming up ideas for Christmas ornaments was simple for Susan Sells. Making them tangible was something else. Sue Bouchard made it all feasible with her knowledge of design and paper piecing. Detailed patterns that aren't usually possible become fun, easy, and quick with this innovative method. Follow your creative stars with the wallhanging and six ornaments we so enjoyed creating. Ornaments are shown on page 82

Ornament size: 4" x 5"
Wallhanging size: 15" x 16"
Patterns provided

Materials

Cut strips selvage to selvage.

Wallhanging

Star

Light (star points & beams)
¼ yd
2" wide strip
3" wide strip
Medium (star center)
⅛ yd
3" wide strip

Kings

Crowns
⅛ yd
2" wide strip
Flesh
⅛ yd
2" wide strip
Gift Boxes
⅛ yd
2" wide strip
Robes (three shades of red, purple & green)
Light (L) red, purple & green
⅛ yd each
2" wide strip each
Medium (M) red, purple & green
⅛ yd each
3" wide strip each
Dark (D) red, purple & green
⅛ yd each
2" wide strip each

Background
¾ yd
three 2" wide strips
two 3" wide strips
8" wide strip

Backing
20" x 22"

Batting
19" x 21"

Binding
¼ yd
two 3" wide strips

Ornaments

Santa
2" - 4" wide strips of various colors

Camel
2" - 3" wide strips of tan and a background color

Rudolph
2" - 4" wide strips of various colors

Angel
2" - 4" wide strips of various colors

Other Materials

"wooden iron"
fabric and paper scissors
trash can

Instructions

Paper piecing is a technique used to easily sew small pieces of fabric together without having to worry about matching seam intersections. The procedure uses a paper pattern foundation on which you use the printed lines as your sewing guide. Work from a central starting point and "build" your patchwork around it. The patterns, Rudolph, Santa, Angel, Star, King and Camel can be used as individual ornaments. Or, as in "Following Yonder Star," combine several to create a small wallhanging.

Fabrics which are solid or appear solid from a distance work best for paper piecing. Large to medium scale prints do not always work. When you cut small pieces from a section of the fabric, you might not get the color you expected or wanted.
Directional prints should only be used when you can visualize the end result. They must be carefully placed before sewing.

General Information for Paper Piecing

1. Make several 100% photocopies of your pattern.

2. Set your machine to 18-20 stitches per inch.

3. Always sew on the printed side of the paper, using the printed line as your guide.

4. Use a larger needle (90/14) to help perforate your paper.

5. All seam allowances should be trimmed back to ⅛".

6. "Unsew" from fabric side, so that you don't tear perforated paper.

Paper Piecing

1. With paper scissors, trim extra paper from pattern sections. Leave at least ¼" around the edge.

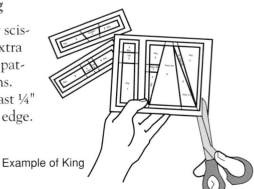

Example of King

2. Cut your first piece of fabric from appropriate size strip to cover area #1. Allow at least ½" around all edges.
It's better to cut the piece large than skimpy.

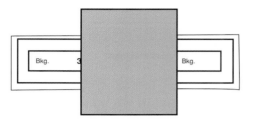

3. Using the light from a window or a light box, position the fabric on the back side of the paper. The wrong side of the fabric should be touching the back side of the paper pattern. Pin in place.

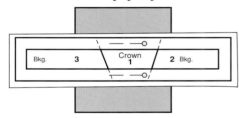

4. On the printed side of the paper pattern, lay the #2 fabric strip over the entire #2 area.

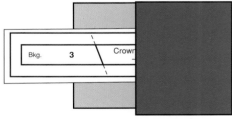

5. Cut piece from strip leaving a extra ½" extending over each end.

6. Lay fabric #2 on table, right side up.

7. Position pattern on top so edge of fabric #2 lies ¼" to right of printed sewing line. Pin.

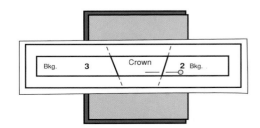

8. Sew on the printed side of line between pieces #1 and #2 with 18-20 stitches per inch.

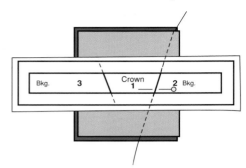

9. Fold paper back along seam line and trim seam allowances to ⅛". *Be careful not to cut the paper.*

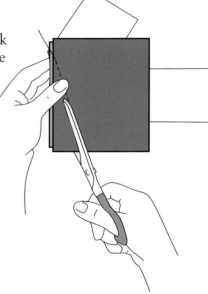

10. Fold fabric #2 open and press seam with a "wooden iron."

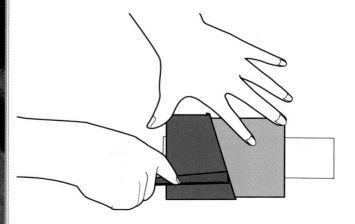

11. Place the next fabric over #3 sewing area with right side up. Cut piece from strip to fit.

12. Without turning the fabric over, move it to the other side of the paper. Line up the raw edge ¼" to the right of the printed sewing line. Pin on the sewing side (printed side of pattern).

13. Sew along line between #3 and the fabrics already in place.

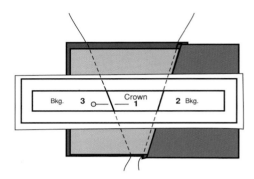

14. Trim seam allowance to ⅛". Fold fabric #3 open.

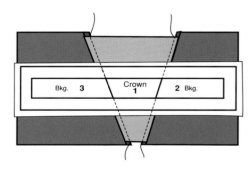

15. Press seam with wooden iron on right side.

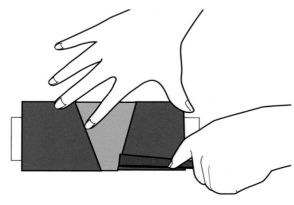

16. Continue in numerical order until all fabrics have been sewn in place.

17. Trim paper and excess fabric back to the ¼" seam allowance.

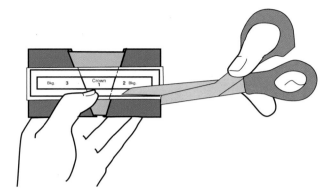

18. Remove paper from back. It is easiest if you start with the highest number and go backwards until you remove the final paper over #1.

19. Pin and sew rows together.

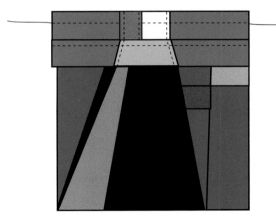

20. Stitch around outside edge ⅛".

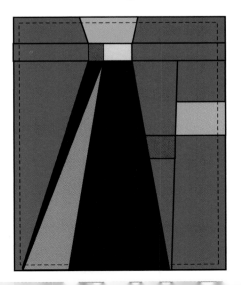

Your patched piece is now ready to finish as an ornament or put together as a small wallhanging.

Ornament: Layer on backing with batting. Machine quilt and finish with a 2" binding. Refer to Finishing instructions, page 112.

Following Yonder Star Wallhanging

1. Cut two background rectangles same size as king block, approximately 4" x 5".

2. Lay out your pieces.

3. Sew top together. See Finishing instructions, page 112.

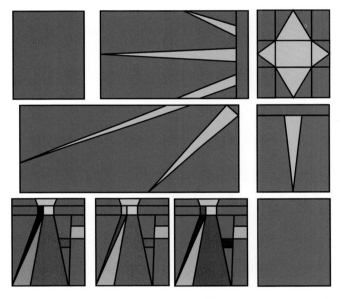

For a more challenging wallhanging, sew together three kings, a camel, the star, and angel.

O Tannenbaum

Grant Burns

$\mathcal{T}$his project is perfect for involving woodworkers in an old fashioned Christmas. Inspired by the sparse feather trees and based on an old custom, this German tree is decorated with bright apples and fragrant gingerbread. I'm always waiting to snag soft cookies that drop from their ribbons.

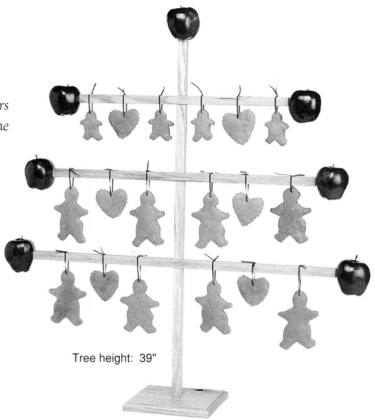

Tree height: 39"

Materials

Tree
¾" x ¾" pine
> 9' or one 36" long for trunk
>> 19" long for branch
>> 24" long for branch
>> 28" long for branch

2" thick pine base
> 8" x 8"

¼" dowel rod
> 36" long
>> Cut into seven 3½" pieces

3" wood screw

Three ⅝" wood screws

Wood stain or oil

Sandpaper
> sheet 100 grit
> sheet 150 grit

Tools needed
> table saw or radial arm saw
> drill
> countersink drill bit
> ¼" drill bit
> screwdriver(s) to fit screws
> pencil sharpener
> wood glue

Instructions

Making the Tree

1. Cut the ¾" x ¾" pine into a 36" section for the trunk, and into 19", 24", and 28" for the branches.

2. In preparation to make lap joints, mark the trunk with a ¾" section starting 4" down, 12" down and 20" down from the top.

3. Mark a ¾" section in the center of the three branches for the lap joints.

4. Adjust your table saw or radial arm saw so that it will cut exactly half of the depth of your trunk and branches.

5. Cut between each ¾" mark by removing the thickness of the blade with each pass. There are 6 total. Remember it's better to remove too little than too much. You can always remove more later to make the joint fit.

6. Drill a ¼" hole 1" deep in the center of the ends of both sides of each branch, and at the top of the trunk.

7. Sharpen one end of the seven 3½" dowel rod sections with a pencil sharpener.

8. Drip glue into each hole at the end of the branches and top of the trunk. Stick the unsharpened end of the dowels into the holes.

9. Drill and countersink 3 holes on the back side of the lap cut outs on the trunk. Make sure the holes match the ⅝" screws.

10. Attach branches to the trunk with the ⅝" screws. Use the 19" branch 4" down from the top, the 24" branch 12" down, and the 28" branch 20" down.

11. Mark the center of the 2" thick base on the bottom by drawing an "X" corner to corner.

12. Drill and countersink a hole at the center of the "X" for the 3" screw to fit through.

13. Extend the screw straight through the center of the bottom of the trunk.

14. Sand and finish with wood stain or oil.

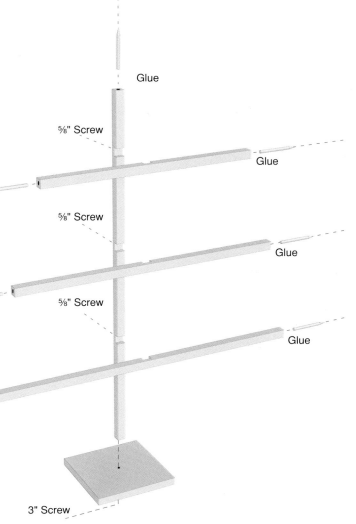

Glue

⅝" Screw

Glue

Glue

⅝" Screw

Glue

Glue

⅝" Screw

Glue

Glue

Glue

3" Screw

Jingle Santa Ornament

LuAnn Stout

*T*his little Santa ornament is easy and fun. Use it for a tree ornament, a package tie, or on a napkin ring. It makes a great gift exchange item.

Ornament size: 5½" long
Pattern provided

Materials

Hat
   3½" x 5½" red print, polka dot, or plaid

Hair
   3½" x 1" white or off white printed muslin

Face
   3½" x 1" beige or pale pink

Beard
   3½" x 3½" same as hair

Interfacing
   3½" x 9" heavyweight fusible interfacing

Back of ornament
   3½" x 9" green print, plaid, or dot

Other Materials

   hat - ½" small red, silver, or gold bell

   eyes - two 4 mm (⅛") black beads

   gold thread - 12"

Instructions

Sewing Directions:

Use ¼" seam allowance and 15 stitches to the inch.

1. Lay out strips in this order:

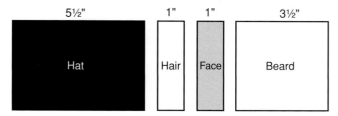

2. Sew together. Press seams toward hat. Piece will measure about 3½" x 9".

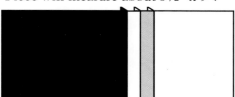

3. Lay the pattern on the sewn strips. Match face, hat, and beard seams with pattern. Cut around pattern.

4. Mark eye positions.

5. Sew beads in place, or eyes can be glued in place at the end of project.

6. Place the rough side of the fusible interfacing to wrong side of backing fabric.

   Press. (Hint: Put a pressing cloth under and over project so iron and board don't get sticky.)

7. Lay pattern on fused backing and cut out.

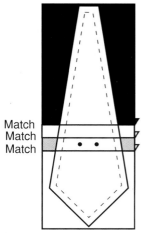

Match
Match
Match

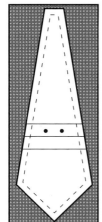

8. Place the fused backing and Santa piece right sides together. Start sewing at the fold line of the hat. Sew around Santa, stopping at the hat to leave an opening for turning.

9. Trim edge ⅛" from the stitching line except at the opening.

10. Turn right side out through opening. Press.

11. Sew bell to hat point.

12. Slip stitch opening shut.

13. Fold Santa's hat down diagonally indicated on pattern. Press.

14. With a needle and gold thread, take a stitch in the seam line at fold of hat.

    Leave a tail of thread. Pull stitch through until thread in needle is same length as tail length. Tie together in a knot. This makes a hanger loop.

    Hang on the tree for all to admire and enjoy!

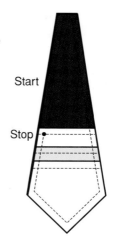

Start

Stop

Twelve Santa Tree Ornaments

Sew 42" strips together for 12 quick and easy gifts or ornaments. Cut your backing into 9" strips and press on interfacing.

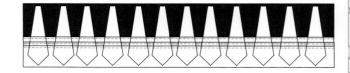

Trace your pattern on the wrong side of the sewn strips, sew ¼" from the line, and then trim.

Scalloped Tree Skirt

LuAnn Stout

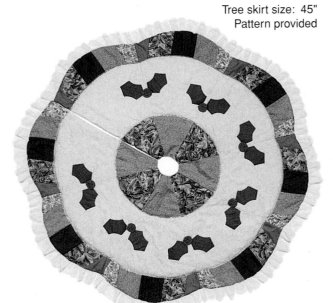

Tree skirt size: 45"
Pattern provided

I love the Christmas season filled with wonderful smells, glorious music, and sparkling lights. It seems that the Christmas season magically transforms everywhere and everything into a fairy land. Best of all for me is the Christmas tree. Now, as well as when I was a child, the tree signals the beginning of this wonderful season of beauty, love, and gift giving. I designed this tree skirt as my gift of beauty and love to you.

Materials Cut strips selvage to selvage.

Background
　1⅛ yd
　　eight gores using pattern

Scallops five assorted fabrics medium and dark
　⅜ yd each
　　4" wide strip from each
　　four 8" squares each from one medium
　　and one dark

Green holly leaves
　¼ yd

Red holly berries
　⅛ yd

Lightweight fusible interfacing
　½ yd
　　two 3½ " wide strips

Braid ½" wide (optional)
　5 yds

Pre-gathered lace 2½" wide (optional)
　4 yds

Backing
　1⅓ yds (must be 45" square)

Thin bonded batting (optional)
　1⅓ yds (must be 45" square)

Other Materials

　template plastic

　invisible thread for machine quilting (optional)

　21" x 20" pattern tracing paper

Instructions

Cutting the Eight Background Gores

1. Fold background fabric in half lengthwise, and half again, so layered fabric is approximately 22" x 20".

2. Place pattern on straight of grain **close to selvage**.

3. Rotary cut through the four thicknesses of fabric along the straight edge of pattern with 6" x 24" ruler. Carefully cut around curved edges. Set gores aside.

4. Place pattern against the cut edge of fabric. Repeat cutting procedure.

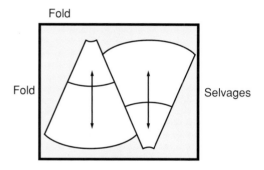

Sewing the Strips for the Curved Patch

1. Lay out the 4" wide strips in desired color order and number them 1-5. One will repeat next to five in finished tree skirt.

2. Sew strips together lengthwise with ¼" seam.

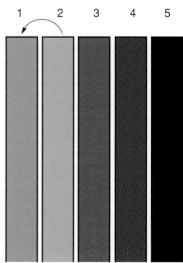

3. Set seams. Press all seams in the same direction toward one.

4. Lay strip set out straight and smooth. Do not fold.

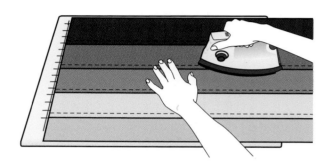

5. Center the curved pattern on the strip set. Each piece must be cut separately so color placement will be correct when sewn to the gore.

6. Carefully cut around pattern. This will be on the curve so handle carefully.

7. Continue cutting eight curved patch pieces.

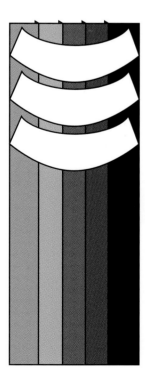

Sewing the Curved Patch Pieces to Gores

1. Match the center of the curved patch piece to the center of the background gore, patch on top. Pin centers. Match the two edges and pin. Carefully pin around the curve.

2. Stitch ¼" from edge. Stretch a little as you sew around the curve.

3. Set the seam and press seam to the patched piece. Trim excess.

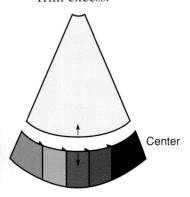

Center

4. Pin two gores right sides together, matching seams at the curved patch piece.

5. Assembly-line sew from small curve to large curve.

6. Set seams. Open gores and press seams to one side.

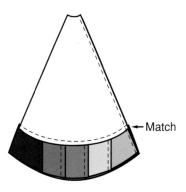

← Match

Cutting Small Wedges

1. Trace wedge pattern from full size pattern.

2. Pair the 8" dark and medium squares right sides together and edges even. Stack.

Wedge

3. Center small wedge pattern on the squares. Cut straight sides with 6" x 12" ruler.

4. Carefully freehand cut around curves.

5. Leave the wedges stacked in pairs, right sides together.

6. Assembly-line sew the pairs together.

7. Clip apart.

8. Set the seams. Open and carefully press seam to the dark side. **Sides are bias, so be careful.** Check to make sure that fabrics alternate when placed together on the large wedge.

9. Place the large curved end of each wedge on a 3½" wide strip of fusible interfacing. The right side of wedge will be against the rough, dotted side of the fusible.

10. Stitch ¼" around the large curved edge of each wedge.

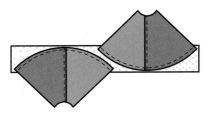

11. Trim seams to ⅛." Turn interfacing to the wrong side of wedge. **Do not press.**

Sewing Wedges to Gores

1. Place one wedge pair right side up onto one gore pair right side up matching the top edge, side edges and the middle sewn seam. Wrong side of wedge will be against right side of gore. Pin. Press the edges where fusible facing is. It will stick in place.

2. Repeat until all four wedge pairs are pinned and pressed to the four gore pairs.

   If you plan to add applique embellishment such as holly and berries, it's easiest to sew them on at this stage.

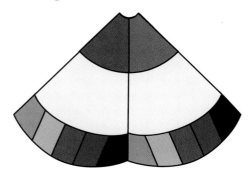

3. Place two gore pairs right sides together. Match seams at wedges and bottom curved patch section. Pin for a perfect match. Sew.

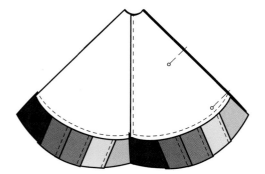

4. Repeat with remaining gore pairs. You will now have two halves with four gores in each half.

5. Place the gored halves right sides together matching at the wedges and bottom curved patch.
   Sew one seam and leave one seam open.

6. *Optional:* Lay braid around the bottom of wedges and along the seam of the curved patch pieces. Stitch. Sew lace around the outside edge.

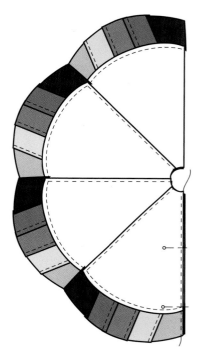

Adding the Holly and Berry (optional)

1. Trace the holly on template plastic and cut out.

2. Trace 14 holly leaf patterns on smooth side of fusible interfacing with a permanent marking pen. Leave ½" between leaves.

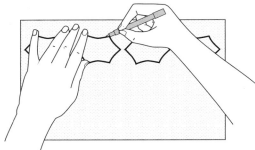

3. Pin the rough side of the fusible interfacing to the right side of the holly fabric. The smooth side of fusible is up.

4. Stitch just inside the drawn line with a small stitch.

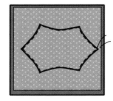

5. Cut between leaves. Trim each piece to ⅛" from the stitching.

6. Pull fusible interfacing away from fabric. Carefully make a small slit through the fusible interfacing only.

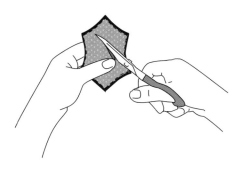

7. Carefully turn right side out. Smooth out curves and poke out points with point turner.

8. Position holly leaves on treeskirt.

9. Press in place.
   Hint: Aluminum foil under the tree skirt will reflect the heat and help the holly stick.

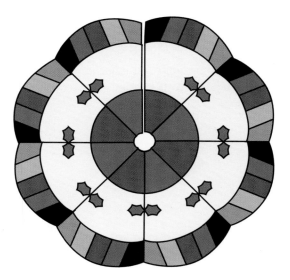

Stitching Holly with Invisible Thread (optional)

1. Thread your machine with invisible thread on top. Loosen top tension. Match the bobbin thread to the background of tree skirt.

2. Stitch around the holly with a blind hem or zigzag stitch.

Stitching Holly with Straight Stitch (optional)

1. Thread your machine with regular, embroidery, top-stitching, or hand quilting thread. Thread can be contrasting or matching.

2. Lengthen stitch to #3 or 10 stitches per inch. Adjust tension if necessary.

3. Stitch around the holly 1/16" from the edge.

Making Yo yo Berries

1. Trace the circle with a 3" diameter on template plastic and cut out.

2. Cut seven circles from berry fabric.

3. Double thread a hand sewing needle with matching thread. Knot the end.

4. Using basting stitches, hand sew around the circle turning under edge ¼" to the wrong side. Pull thread tight, push needle to the back and knot.

5. Bar tack yo yo's in place through all the layers after the tree skirt is finished.

Other Decorating Options

In place of the holly and berry decorations, other choices include: Angel, page 56,
Poinsettia, page 70,
Beary Christmas, page 71,
Snowman, page 24.

Adding the Backing

1. Lay the backing out flat right side up. *Optional:* place batting **underneath**.

2. Place gored tree skirt to the backing right sides together. Pin around outside circle, sides, and inside circle.

3. Stitch around outside edge, leaving a 12" opening along one side. Trim away backing and optional batting. Clip seam allowances along inside and outside curves for easier turning.

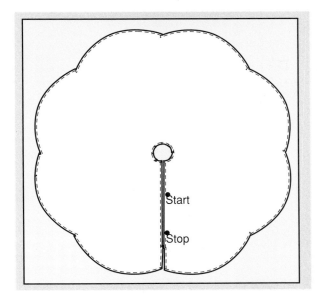

Finishing the Tree Skirt

1. Pin and slip stitch opening closed.

2. Stitch around the wedge circle with your choice of:

    a. invisible thread and blind hem stitch or

    b. matching thread and topstitch

3. "Stitch in the ditch" around the curved pieces.

Every holiday my family and I sit down to a candle light dinner. This tradition, passed on to us by family friend and author Emilee Barnes, is to lit candles clipped to our plates. At the end of the meal each of us in turn expresses what we are grateful for or how life has been blessed. Then the person blows out the candle. Each takes a turn until all the candles are

Dana Butler

Our neighborhood of five families had a progressive family Christmas dinner party. Ea family had a part of the dinner at their house. The last house had the games. As we walked from house to house we sang Christmas carols along the way.

The favorite main dish was Beef Barbecu The evening always ended with the children's favorite game, "Murder in the Dark." This party was the favorite holiday event for everyor Even the college students would ask their families to wait until they got home to have the Neighborhood Christmas party.

Barbecue Beef

5 lbs roast beef sliced and cooked

2 tbsp fat

2 onions chopped

2 cups chopped celery

1 large green pepper chopped

Brown in fat and then add:

2 tbsp sugar

1 tsp lemon juice

1 tbsp vinegar

1 tbsp worcestershire sauce

1 tsp dry mustard

Salt, paprika, and pepper to taste

Add ½ cup catsup or tomatoes and ½ cup chili sauce or salsa.

Simmer until thick. Serve on hamburger buns. Serves about 15.

LuAnn Stout

Holiday Table

Candle Placemats

Pat Wetzel

Placemat size:
14" x 18"

C reate six easy holiday placemats using flying geese patches. They will add beauty to your Christmas table or make great gifts for friends or family.

Materials Cut strips selvage to selvage.

Print
1/3 yd
two 5¼"wide strips
twelve 5¼" squares

Background
1½ yds
two 6½" wide strips
twelve 6½" squares
2⅞" wide strip
twelve 2⅞" squares
two 2½" wide strips
(24) 1½" x 2½"
and six 2½" x 4½"
4½" wide strip
six 4½" x 6½"
two 10½" wide strips
six 10½" x your size candle height

Gold lamé, backed
6" x 8"
twelve 1⅞" squares

Fleece
1½ yds
six 18" x 22" pieces

Backing
1½ yds
three 18" wide strips
six 18" x 22"

Binding
⅞ yd
twelve 2½" wide strips

Instructions

Making Forty-eight Flying Geese Patches

1. Center 5¼" print square on the 6½" background square right sides together.

2. Press. Draw diagonal line across the squares from corner to corner. Pin.

3. Assembly-line sew ¼" on each side of the line. It is important to be accurate. Press.

4. Cut apart on line.

5.

Press open with the seam allowance toward the larger triangle.

6. Place the squares right sides together with opposite fabrics touching. The outside edges will meet, but the seams will not meet. Press.

7. Draw diagonal line from corner to corner across the seam. Pin.

8. Assembly-line sew ¼" on each side of the line. It is important to be accurate. Press.

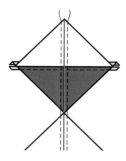

9. Cut apart on the line. Clip between the seams to the stitching.

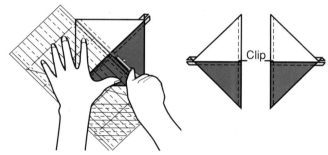

10. Press the squares open, pushing the seam allowance toward the larger triangle.

11. Cut each block in half, leaving a ¼" seam allowance above each peak.

12. Trim out (48) Flying Geese patches to 2½" x 4½".

   Place ruler on top. Center the peak at 2¼" (halfway along the 4½" measurement). Trim on two sides. Turn block. Trim on remaining two sides.

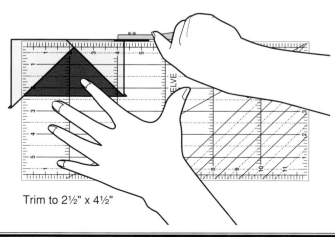

Trim to 2½" x 4½"

Making Twelve Flame Patches

Be sure to purchase lamé with backing.

1. Cut the twelve 2⅞" background squares on both diagonals to make (48) triangles.

2. Center and sew a triangle to one side of the 1⅞" flame square. Assembly-line sew a triangle to twelve flame squares. Fingerpress open, seam allowance away from flame.

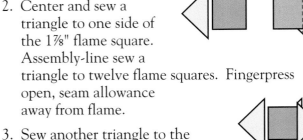

3. Sew another triangle to the opposite side. Fingerpress open, seam allowance away from flame.

4. Center and sew triangles to remaining sides.

5. Press gently with cool iron.

6. Square to 2½", preserving ¼" seam allowance beyond each flame point. See circle.

Sewing the Sides and Top to the Flames

1. Sew 1½" x 2½" background piece to left and right sides of all twelve flame patches.

2. Press seam allowances away from center.

3. Divide flame patches into two equal stacks of six each.

4. Lay out six 2½" x 4½" background pieces with one stack of flame patches for the tall candles.

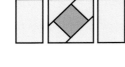

Lay out six 6½" x 4½" background pieces with remaining stack of flame patches for the short candles.

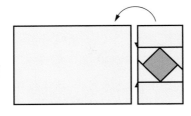

5. Sew background pieces to flame patches.

6. Press seam allowance away from flame.

Sewing Eighteen Flying Geese Pairs

1. Set aside twelve Flying Geese patches.

2. Sew remaining 36 Flying Geese patches into 18 pairs.

Making Six Tall Candles

1. In stacks of six lay out two Flying Geese pairs with a single Flying Geese patch and the smaller flame patch.

2.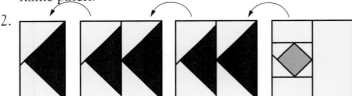

Assembly-line sew candles.

3. Press seam allowances away from flame.

Making Six Short Candles

1. In stacks of six lay out a Flying Geese pair with a single Flying Geese patch and larger flame patch.

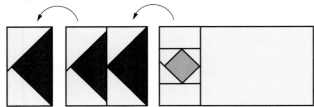

2. Assembly-line sew candles.

3. Press seam allowances away from flame.

Sewing the Top Together

1. Sliver trim the sides of all candles to the same width, approximately 4½", preserving the ¼" seam allowance.

2. Measure the height of the tall candles and the short candles. If they differ, trim top edge to the same height, approximately 14½".

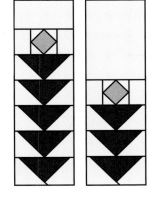

3. Cut 10½" wide background strips into six placemat centers, 10½" wide by your candle height measurement.

4. In stacks of six lay out placemat centers and short candle.

5. Assembly-line sew, being careful to sew across where seams meet.

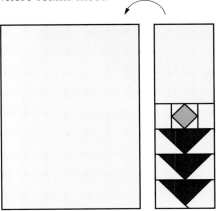
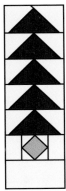

6. Assembly-line sew tall candles to placemats.

7. Press seam allowances away from candles.

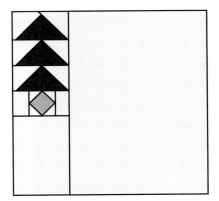

Machine Quilting

1. Use a marker that can be removed. Mark diagonal quilting lines 2" apart.

   Start with lines corner to corner. (see dark lines) Continue diagonal lines across top of flame.

2. Lay out backing pieces, right side down. Layer with fleece and placemat, right side up. Pin.

3. Match bobbin thread to backing fabric. Use invisible thread or your choice thread in the top.

4. Sew with a large stitch, 10 to the inch.

   See Finishing instructions, page 112.

Ribbon Rose Napkin Ring

Eleanor Burns

*C*hristmas dinner is my favorite! I love to prepare turkey with all
the trimmings, fill my dining room with guests, and then serve
dinner on holiday china. As a special party favor, guests love their
Christmas Rose, first as a decorative napkin ring, and then as a
fancy boutonniere before gravy gets spilled on it!

A symbol of love, Christmas roses are quick and easy to make.

Materials

Rose

  30" of 1" – 1½" wide French wire ribbon

Leaves

  10" of ⅝" wide French wire ribbon

Bow

  28" of ⅝" wide French wire ribbon

Other Materials

pin clasp

low temperature glue gun

cloth napkin

Instructions

Use ribbon roses to embellish a vest, decorate the Christmas tree or packages.

Rose

1. Tie a knot in one end; pull taut.

2. Poke copper wire end out along one side at opposite end.

3. Loosely gather ribbon along this wire down to knot.

4. Continue gathering until entire side is ruffled and curling naturally. Leave wire end free, do not cut off.

5. Begin to shape rose by wrapping ruffled ribbon around knot.

6. Wrap tightly at first to form a "bud," then fold over several inches to shape around bud.

7. Continue wrapping loosely so that rose flares out into an open flower shape.

8. At end, fold raw edge down to meet gathered edge.

9. Secure rose by catching free end with wire and wrapping around knot tightly; cut off wire end. Adjust rose "petals" as needed by ruffling, hand stitching, or crumpling as desired.

Leaves

1. Cut 10" piece into two 5" pieces.

2. Fold 5" piece in half.

3. Pull one wire from each end toward center, being careful not to pull the wires through.

4. Twist wire ends to lock.

5. Open leaf and flatten.

6. Twist tip of leaf.

7. Sew or glue leaf to flower.

8. Glue a pin clasp on back.

9. Fold the napkin. Tie the 28" piece around the napkin into a bow.

10. Pin the rose on the bow.

Pine Tree Table Runner

Sue Bouchard

$\mathcal{T}$he Christmas tree is often the center of many family holiday celebrations. Now you can decorate your table with a Pine Tree table runner which will look good from either side of the table. You can also make the table runner in alternate color combinations for any time of the year. This is a great centerpiece for mountain homes or cabins.

Table runner size: 14" x 50"

Materials

Cut strips selvage to selvage. Avoid directional prints.

Tree green
    ½ yd
        7½" wide strip
            five 7½" squares
            cut one more 7½" square

Red
    ½ yd
        three 9" squares
        3" wide strip
            two 3" x 20"

Tree trunk brown
    ⅛ yd
        1½" wide strip
            two 1½" x 20"

Light background
    ½ yd
        three 9" squares
        3" wide strip
            two 3" x 20"

Border
    ¼ yd
        three 1½" wide strips

Binding
    ⅜ yd
        four 3" wide strips

Backing
    ⅞ yd
        cut in half on fold,
        seam to make one long piece

Thin dense batting
    20" x 60"

Instructions

Making Twelve Tree Patches with Green and Light

1. Right sides together, center a 7½" green square on a 9" light square.

2. Press. Draw a diagonal line exactly across the squares from corner to corner. Pin.

 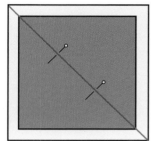

3. Sew ¼" from both sides of drawn line. Press.

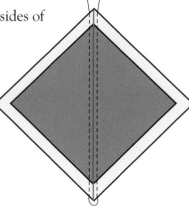

4. Cut on the line.

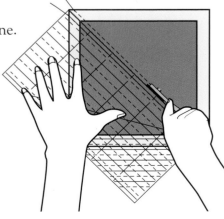

5. Press the pieces open, seam allowance toward the larger triangle.

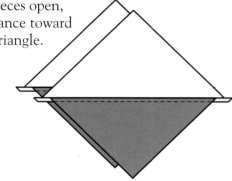

6. Place the squares right sides together with opposite fabrics touching. Notice that the seams do not meet. Match the outside edges.

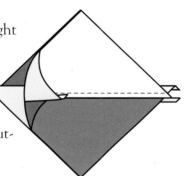

7. Press. Draw a diagonal line from corner to corner, crossing the seams. To ensure a good right angle, place a ruler line on the stitching when drawing.

8. Pin. Sew ¼" from both sides of drawn line.

9. Press. Cut on the line.

10. Clip between the seams to the stitching in order to press both seam allowances toward the larger triangles.

Clip

11. Press each square open, pushing seam allowances toward the larger triangles.

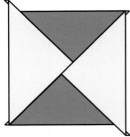

12. Cut each block in half, leaving a ¼" seam allowance above each peak.

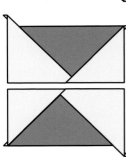

13. Place ruler on top. Center the peak at 3¼", half way along the 6½" measurement.

14. Trim four tree patches to 3½" x 6½". (*Trim on two sides. Turn block. Trim on remaining two sides.*)

15. Repeat with two more sets of green and light for a total of twelve patches.

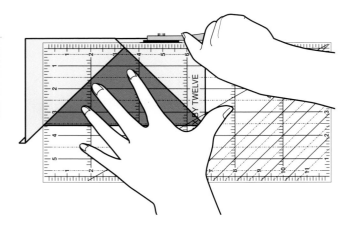

Making Twelve Tree Patches with Green and Red

Repeat method, using 7½" green squares on 9" red squares. Trim to 3½" x 6½".

Making Four Trunk Patches with Trunk and Light

1. Sew strips together.

2. Press seam allowances toward the trunk.

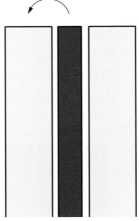

3. Compare the width of the sewn strips with the width of your tree patches. They should be the same.

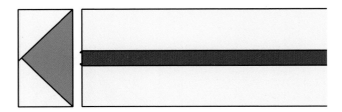

If the trunk strips are wider, trim from both sides to fit.

If the trunk strips are too narrow, resew with a smaller seam allowance.

4. Trim selvages and straighten left end.

5. Cut four 3½" by 6½" patches.

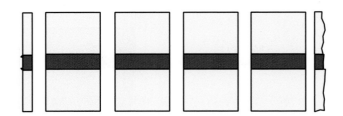

Making Four Trunk Patches with Trunk and Red

Repeat method, using trunk and red strips.

Separate your tree patches and trunk patches into stacks of light background and red background.

Making Four Light Tree Blocks

1. Lay out three stacks of four tree patches and one stack of trunk patches.

2. Flip stack 2 piece to stack 1 piece. Sew. Assembly-line sew stacks.

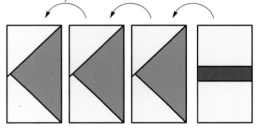

3. Open and add stack 3, and stack 4.

4. Press the block seams toward the top of the four trees.

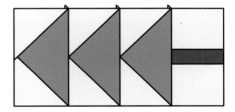

Making Four Red Tree Blocks

Repeat method, using red pieces.

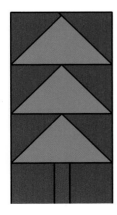

Sewing the Blocks Together

Lay out your blocks, alternating both the color and direction. Please note that all the trees with the same color background will be going the same way.

See Finishing instructions on page 112.

Finishing Quilts and Wallhangings

Piecing Borders and Binding Strips

1. Stack and square off the ends of each strip, trimming away the selvage edges.

2. Seam the strips of each fabric into long pieces by assembly-line sewing. Lay the first strip right side up. Lay the second strip right sides to it. Backstitch, stitch the short ends together, and backstitch again.

3. Take the strip on the top and fold it so the right side is up.

4. Place the third strip right sides to it, backstitch, stitch, and backstitch again.

5. Continue assembly-line sewing all the short ends together into long pieces for each fabric.

6. Clip the threads holding the strips together.

7. Press seams to one side.

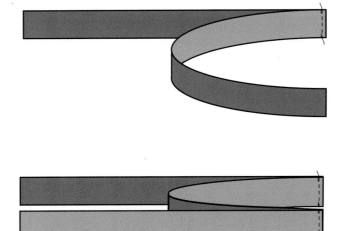

Sewing the Borders to the Quilt Top

1. Measure down the center to find the length. Cut two side strips that measurement plus two inches.

2. Right sides together, match and pin the center of the strips to the center of the sides. Pin at ends, allowing an extra inch of border at each end. Pin intermittently. Sew with the quilt on top. "Set and direct the seams," pressing toward the borders.

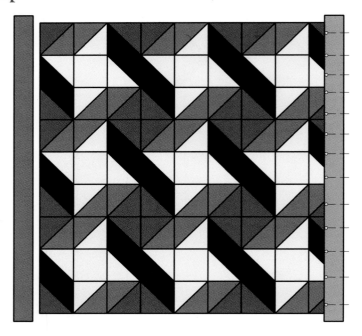

3. Square the ends even with the top and bottom of the quilt.

4. Measure the width across the center including newly added borders. Cut two strips that measurement plus two inches.

5. Right sides together, match and pin the center of the strips to the center of the top and bottom edges of the quilt. Pin at the ends, allowing an extra inch of border at both ends. Pin intermittently. Sew with the quilt on top.

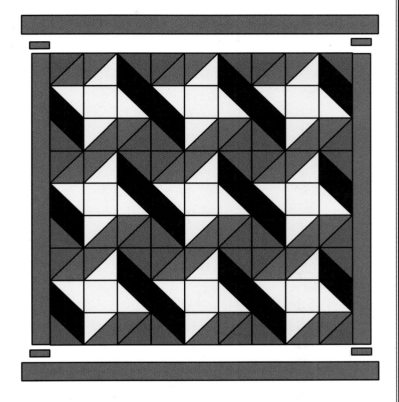

6. "Set and direct the seams," pressing toward the borders. Square the ends even with the side borders.

    Repeat these steps for additional borders.

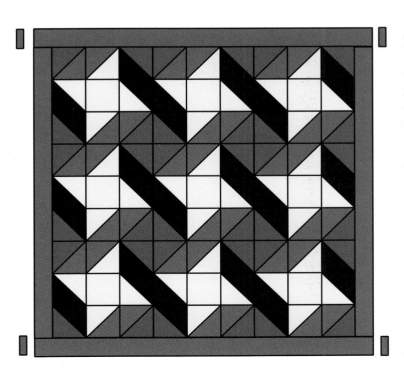

Machine Quilting

Layering Quilt Top or Wallhanging with Backing and Batting

1. Piece the backing yardage together for larger size quilts.

2. Stretch out the backing right side down on a table or floor. Tape down on a floor area or clamp onto a table with large binder clips.

3. Place and smooth out the batting on top. Lay the quilt top right side up and centered on top of the batting. Completely smooth and stretch all layers until they are flat. Tape or clip securely. The backing and batting should extend at least 2" on all sides.

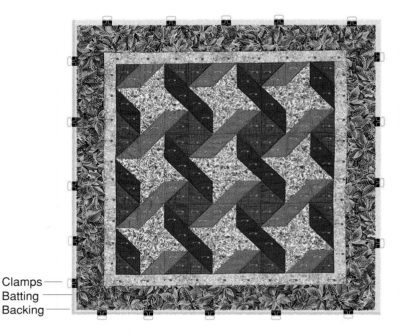

Clamps
Batting
Backing

Marking the Quilt Top

Decide where you want the quilting lines. With the 6" x 24" ruler, lightly mark the lines for machine quilting. Use chalk, a thin dry sliver of soap, a hera tool, or a silver pencil. Make certain that you can remove the marks from the fabric.

Quick and Easy Safety Pinning

Place safety pins throughout the quilt away from the marked quilting lines. Begin pinning in the center and work to the outside, spacing them every 5".

Grasp the opened pin in your right hand and the pinning tool in your left hand. Push the pin through the three layers, and bring the tip of the pin back out. Catch the tip in the groove of the tool and allow point to extend far enough to push pin closure down.

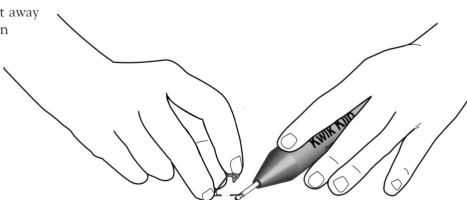

Machine Quilting the Marked Lines

Use a walking foot attachment for straight line quilting. Use invisible thread in the top of your machine and regular thread in the bobbin to match the backing. Loosen the top tension, and lengthen your stitch to 8 - 10 stitches per inch, or a #3 or #4 setting. Free arm machines need the "bed" placed for more surface area.

1. Trim the backing and batting to within 2" of the outside edge of the quilt.

2. Roll the quilt tightly from the outside edge in toward middle. Hold this roll with clips or pins.

3. Slide this roll into the keyhole of the sewing machine.

4. Place the needle in the depth of the seam and pull up the bobbin thread. Lock the beginning and ending of each quilting line by backstitching.

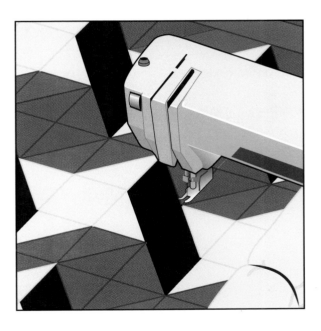

5. Place your hands flat on both sides of the needle to form a hoop. Keep the quilt area flat and tight. If you need to ease in the top fabric, feed the quilt through the machine by pushing the layers of fabric and batting forward underneath the walking foot.

6. If puckering occurs, remove stitching by grasping the bobbin thread with a pin or tweezers and pull gently to expose the invisible thread. Touch the invisible thread stitches with the rotary cutter blade as you pull the bobbin thread free from the quilt.

7. Unroll, roll, and machine quilt on all lines, sewing the length or width or diagonal of the quilt.

Adding the Binding

See Piecing Strips, page 112.

Use a walking foot attachment and regular thread on top and in the bobbin to match the binding. Use 10 stitches per inch, or #3 setting.

1. Press the binding strip in half lengthwise with right sides out.

2. Line up the raw edges of the folded binding with the raw edge of the quilt top at the middle of one side.

3. Begin sewing 4" from the end of the binding.

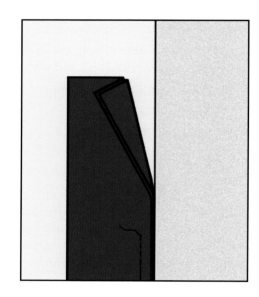

4. At the corner, stop the stitching ¼" from the edge with the needle in the fabric. Raise the presser foot and turn the quilt to the next side. Put the foot back down.

5. Sew backwards ¼" to the edge of the binding, raise the foot, and pull the quilt forward slightly.

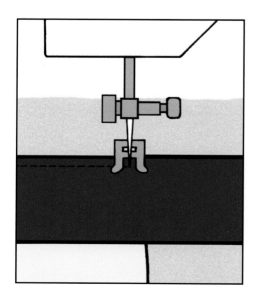

6. Fold the binding strip straight up on the diagonal. Fingerpress in the diagonal fold.

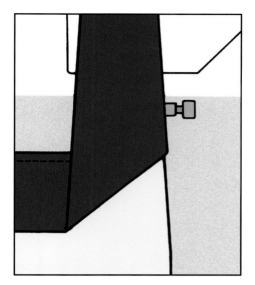

7. Fold the binding strip straight down with the diagonal fold underneath. Line up the top of the fold with the raw edge of the binding underneath.

8. Begin sewing from the corner.

9. Continue sewing and mitering the corners around the outside of the quilt.

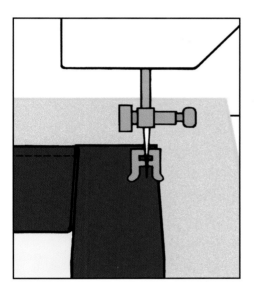

10. Stop sewing 4" from where the ends will overlap.

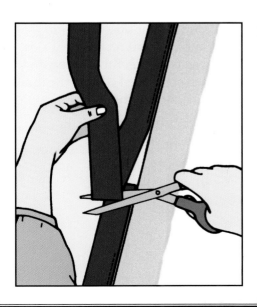

11. Line up the two ends of binding. Trim the excess with a ½" overlap. Open out the folded ends and pin right sides together. Sew a ¼" seam.

12. Continue to sew the binding in place.

13. Trim the batting and backing up to the raw edges of the binding.

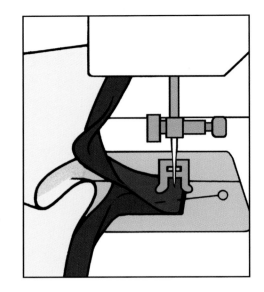

14. Fold the binding to the backside of the quilt. Pin in place so that the folded edge on the binding covers the stitching line. Tuck in the excess fabric at each miter on the diagonal.

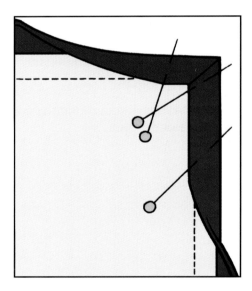

15. From the right side, "stitch in the ditch" using invisible thread on the right side, and a bobbin thread to match the binding on the back side. Catch the folded edge of the binding on the back side with the stitching.

    Optional: Hand slip stitch.

16. Sew an idetntification label on the back listing your name, date, and other pertinent information.

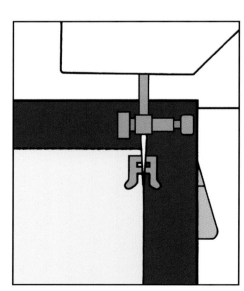

Acknowledgements

Poinsettias to Gerri Skegstad for Christmas settings she created for photo sessions in her beautiful home.

Holly and Mistletoe to designers and staff at Quilt in a Day for contributions and dedication to "Christmas Quilts and Crafts."

Index

Order Information

Quilt in a Day books offer a wide range of techniques and are directed toward a variety of skill levels. If you do not have a quilt shop in your area, you may write for a complete catalog and current price list of all books and patterns published by Quilt in a Day®, Inc., 1955 Diamond Street, San Marcos, CA 92069 or call to order toll free 1 800 777-4852 between the hours of 8 am – 5 pm Pacific Time.

Easy

These books are easy enough for beginners of any age.
Quilt in a Day Log Cabin
Irish Chain in a Day
Bits & Pieces Quilt
Trip Around the World Quilt
Heart's Delight Wallhanging
Scrap Quilt, Strips and Spider Webs
Rail Fence Quilt
Dresden Placemats
Flying Geese Quilt
Star for all Seasons Placemats
Winning Hand Quilt
Courthouse Steps Quilt
From Blocks to Quilt

Applique

While these offer a variety of techniques, easy applique is featured in each.
Applique in a Day
Dresden Plate Quilt
Sunbonnet Sue Visits Quilt in a Day
Recycled Treasures
Country Cottages and More
Creating with Color
Spools & Tools Wallhanging
Dutch Windmills Quilt

Intermediate to Advanced

With a little Quilt in a Day experience, these books offer a rewarding project.
Trio of Treasured Quilts
Lover's Knot Quilt
Amish Quilt
May Basket Quilt
Morning Star Quilt
Friendship Quilt

Tulip Quilt
Star Log Cabin Quilt
Burgoyne Surrounded Quilt
Bird's Eye Quilt
Snowball Quilt
Tulip Table Runner

Holiday

Country Christmas
Bunnies & Blossoms
Patchwork Santa
Last Minute Gifts
Angel of Antiquity
Log Cabin Wreath Wallhanging
Log Cabin Christmas Tree Wallhanging
Country Flag
Lover's Knot Placemats

Sampler

Always and forever popular are books with a variety of patterns.
The Sampler
Block Party Series 1, Quilter's Year
Block Party Series 2, Baskets & Flowers
Block Party Series 3, Quilters Almanac
Block Party Series 4, Christmas Traditions
Block Party Series 5, Pioneer Sampler

Angle Piecing

Quilt in a Day "template free" methods make angle cutting less of a challenge.
Diamond Log Cabin Tablecloth or Treeskirt
Pineapple Quilt
Blazing Star Tablecloth
Schoolhouse Quilt
Radiant Star Quilt

Paper Piecing Star

Photocopy at 100%

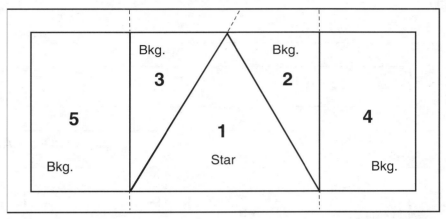

Section A

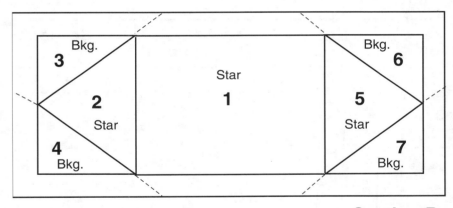

Section B

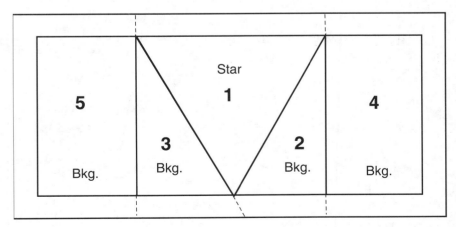

Section C

Paper Piecing King
Photocopy at 100%

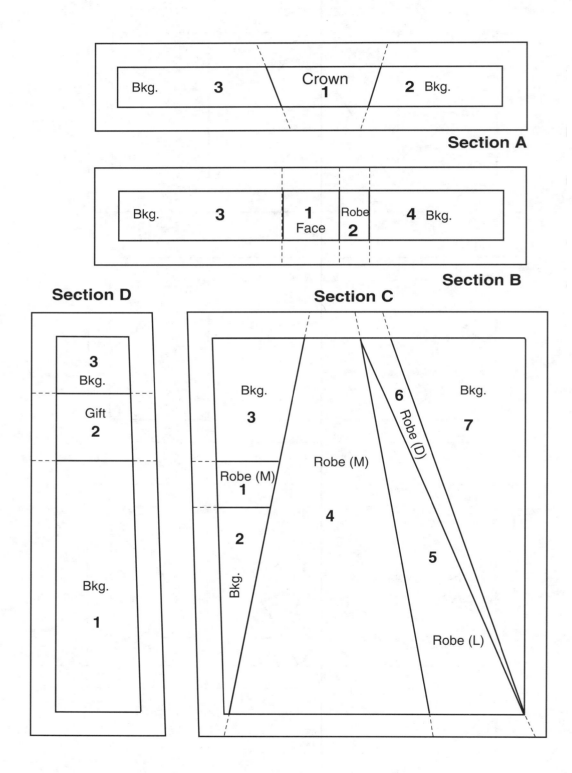

Bkg. **3** Crown **1** **2** Bkg.

Section A

Bkg. **3** **1** Face Robe **2** **4** Bkg.

Section B

Section D

Section C

3 Bkg.

Gift **2**

Bkg. **1**

Bkg. **3**

Robe (M) **1**

2

Bkg.

Robe (M) **4**

6 Robe (D)

Bkg. **7**

5

Robe (L)

Paper Piecing Camel
Photocopy at 100%

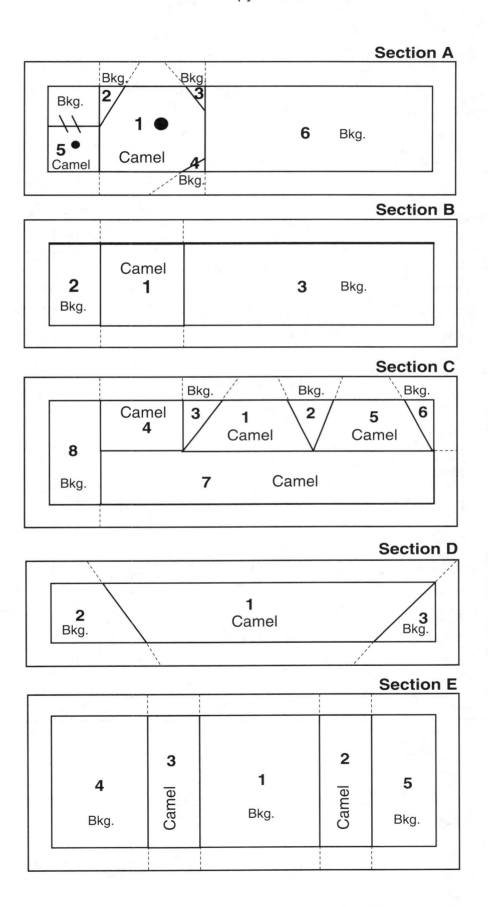

Section A

Bkg. — Bkg.

Bkg.

2

3

1 ●

5 ●
Camel

Camel

4
Bkg.

6 Bkg.

Section B

2
Bkg.

Camel
1

3 Bkg.

Section C

Camel
4

Bkg. — **3** — **1** — Bkg. — **2** — **5** — Bkg. — **6**

Camel

Camel

8
Bkg.

7 Camel

Section D

2
Bkg.

1
Camel

3
Bkg.

Section E

4

Bkg.

3

Camel

1

Bkg.

2

Camel

5

Bkg.

Paper Piecing Background 2
Photocopy at 100%

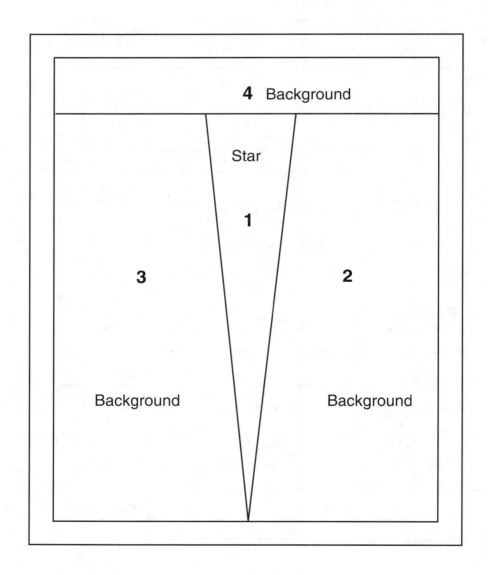

4 Background

Star

1

3

2

Background

Background

Paper Piecing Background 3

Photocopy at 100%

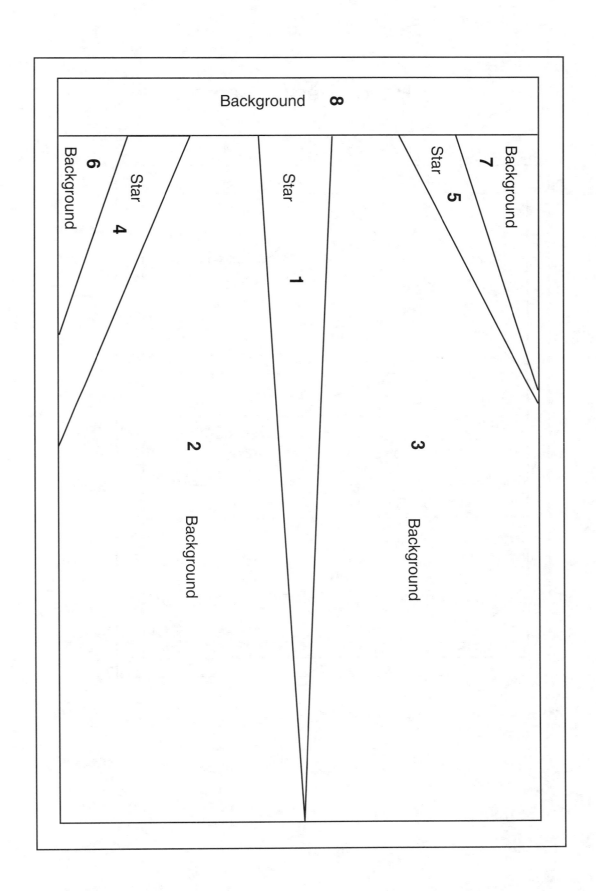

Paper Piecing Santa

Photocopy at 100%

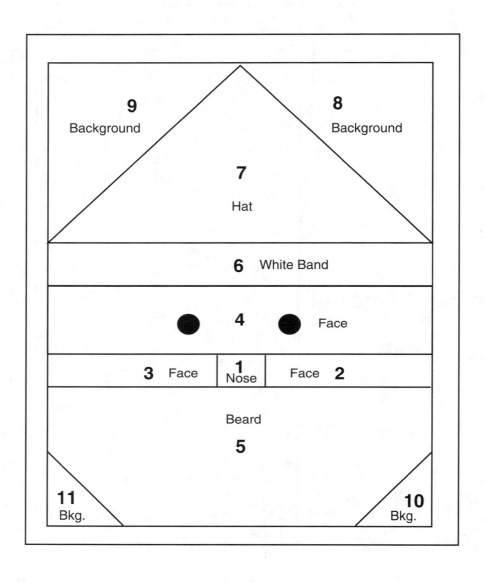

Paper Piecing Angel

Photocopy at 100%

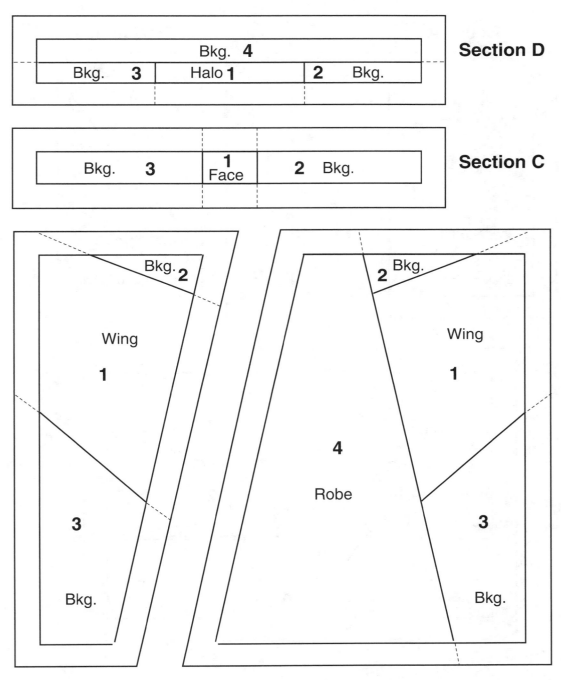

Section D

Bkg. **4**

Bkg. **3**   Halo **1**   **2**   Bkg.

Section C

Bkg. **3**   **1** Face   **2**   Bkg.

Bkg. **2**

Wing **1**

3

Bkg.

Section A

2 Bkg.

Wing **1**

4

Robe

3

Bkg.

Section B

Paper Piecing Rudolph

Photocopy at 100%

Section A

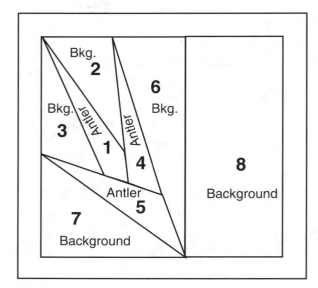

Bkg. **2**

6 Bkg.

Bkg. **3**

Antler

Antler

1

4

Antler **5**

8 Background

7 Background

Section B

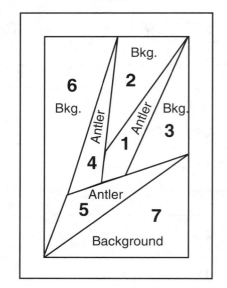

Bkg. **2**

6 Bkg.

Antler

Antler

1

Bkg. **3**

4

Antler **5**

7 Background

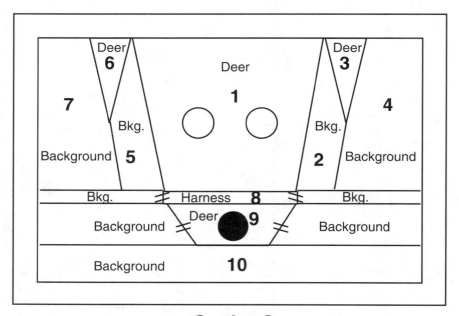

Deer **6**

Deer

1

Deer **3**

7

Bkg. **5**

Background

Bkg. **2**

4

Background

Bkg. Harness **8** Bkg.

Background Deer **9** Background

Background **10**

Section C

Wintertime Friends

Trace

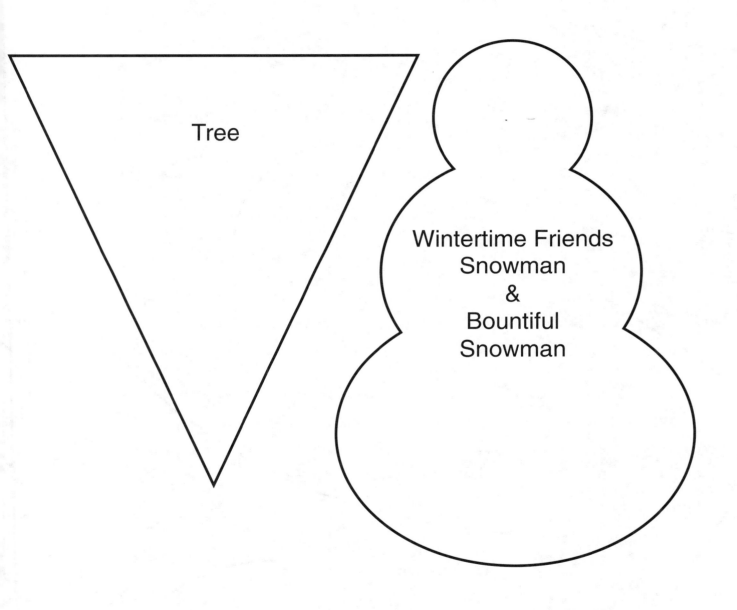

Tree

Wintertime Friends
Snowman
&
Bountiful
Snowman

Star Catcher Angel

Trace

1

2

3

3

4

5

6

7

Stained Glass Wreath
Patterns

Trace

Stained Glass Wreath
Patterns

Trace

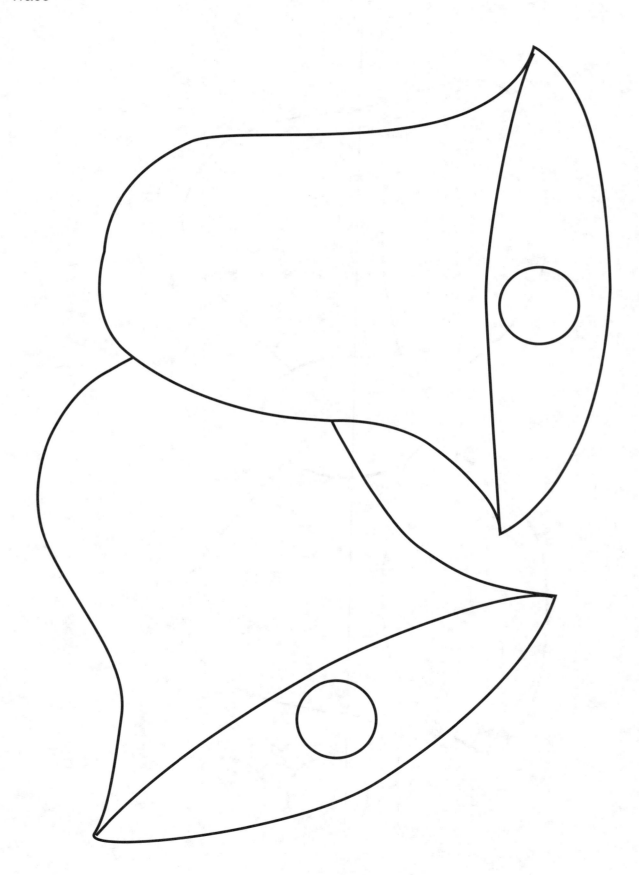

Poinsettia Wallhanging

Trace

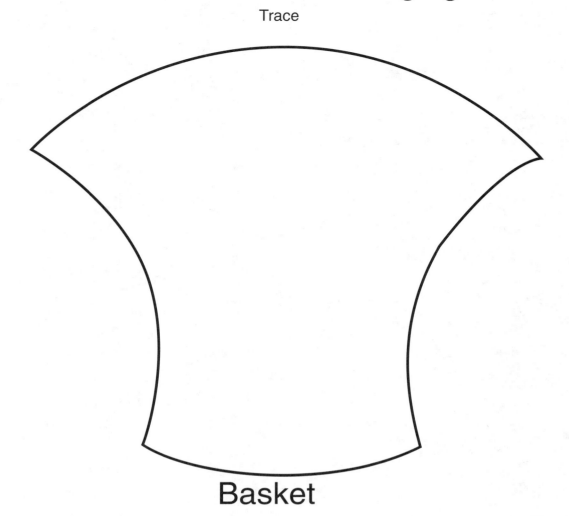

Basket

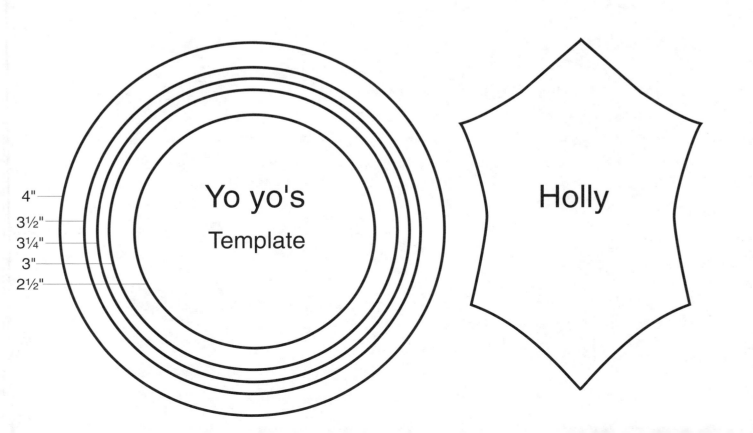

4"

3½"

3¼"

3"

2½"

Yo yo's

Template

Holly

Jingle Santa Ornament

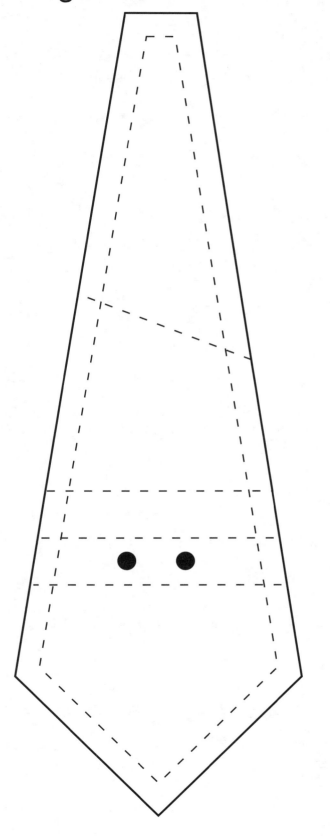

Following Yonder Star
Background 1
Photocopy at 100%

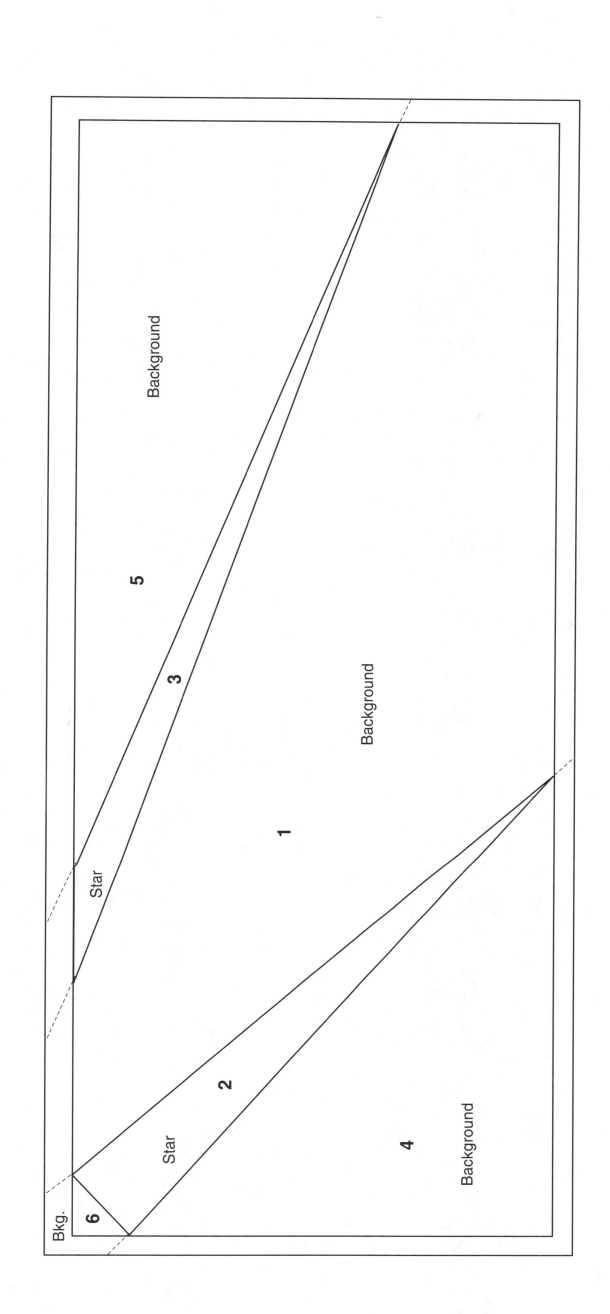

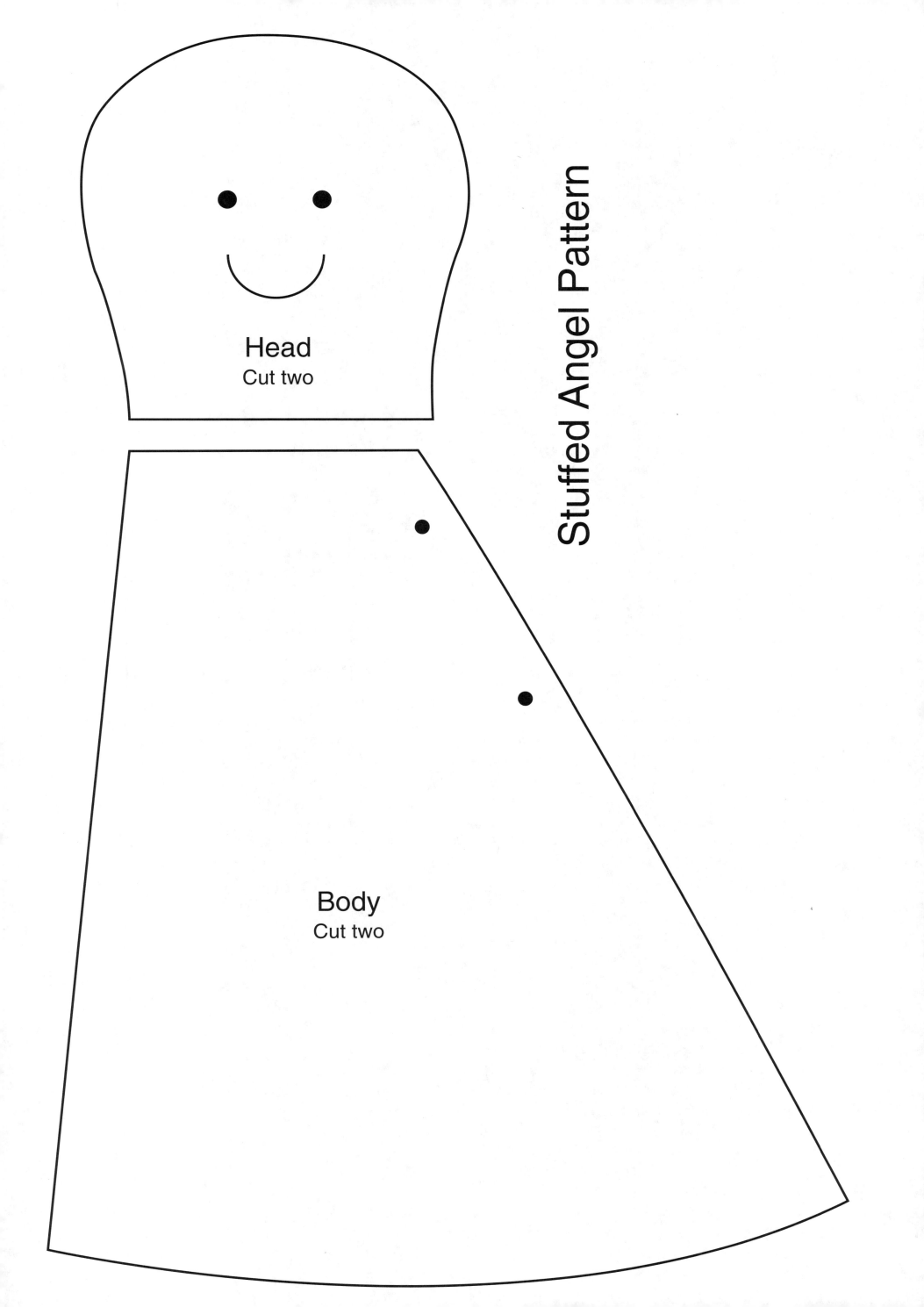

Head
Cut two

Body
Cut two

Stuffed Angel Pattern

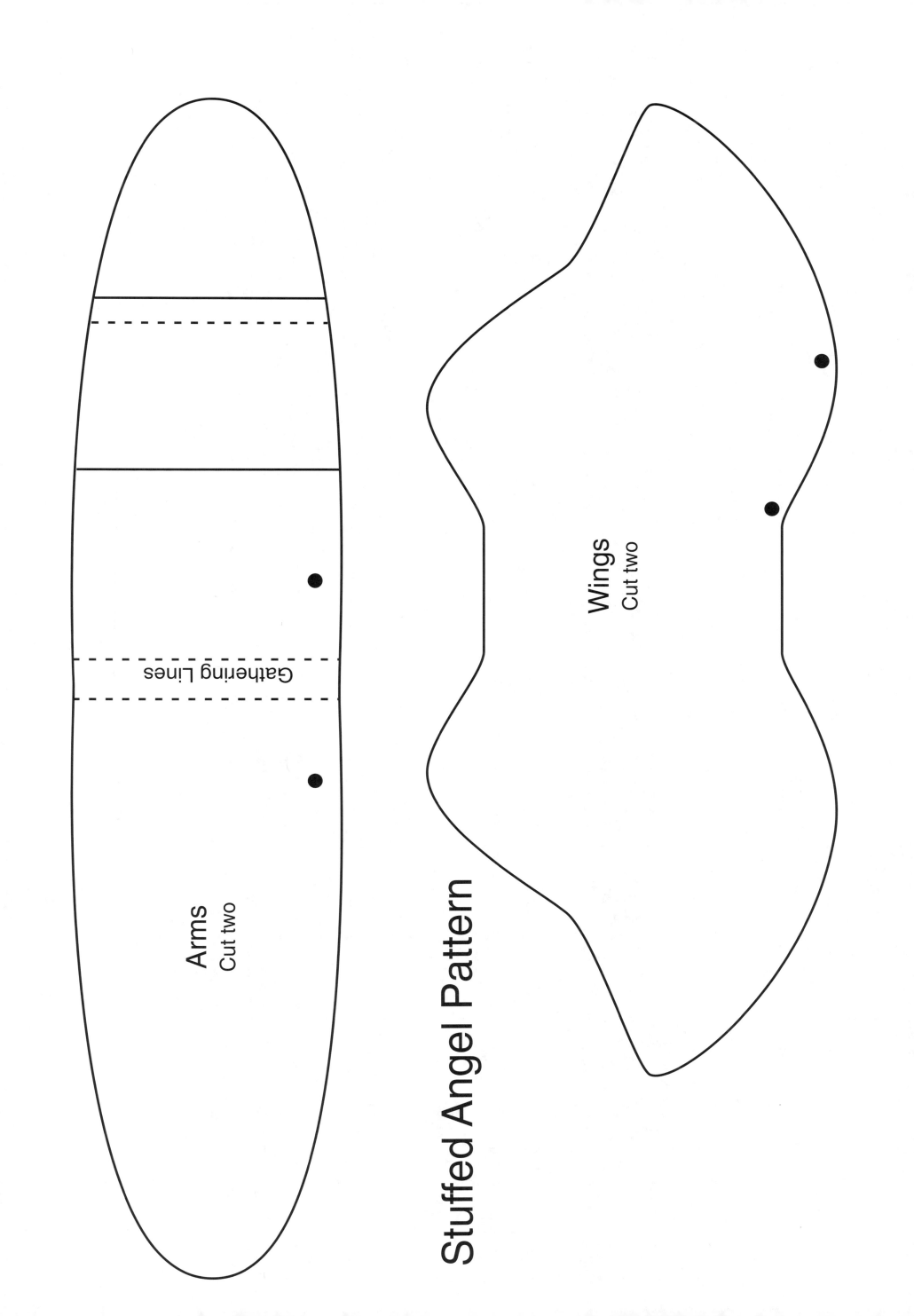

Arms
Cut two

Gathering Lines

Wings
Cut two

Stuffed Angel Pattern

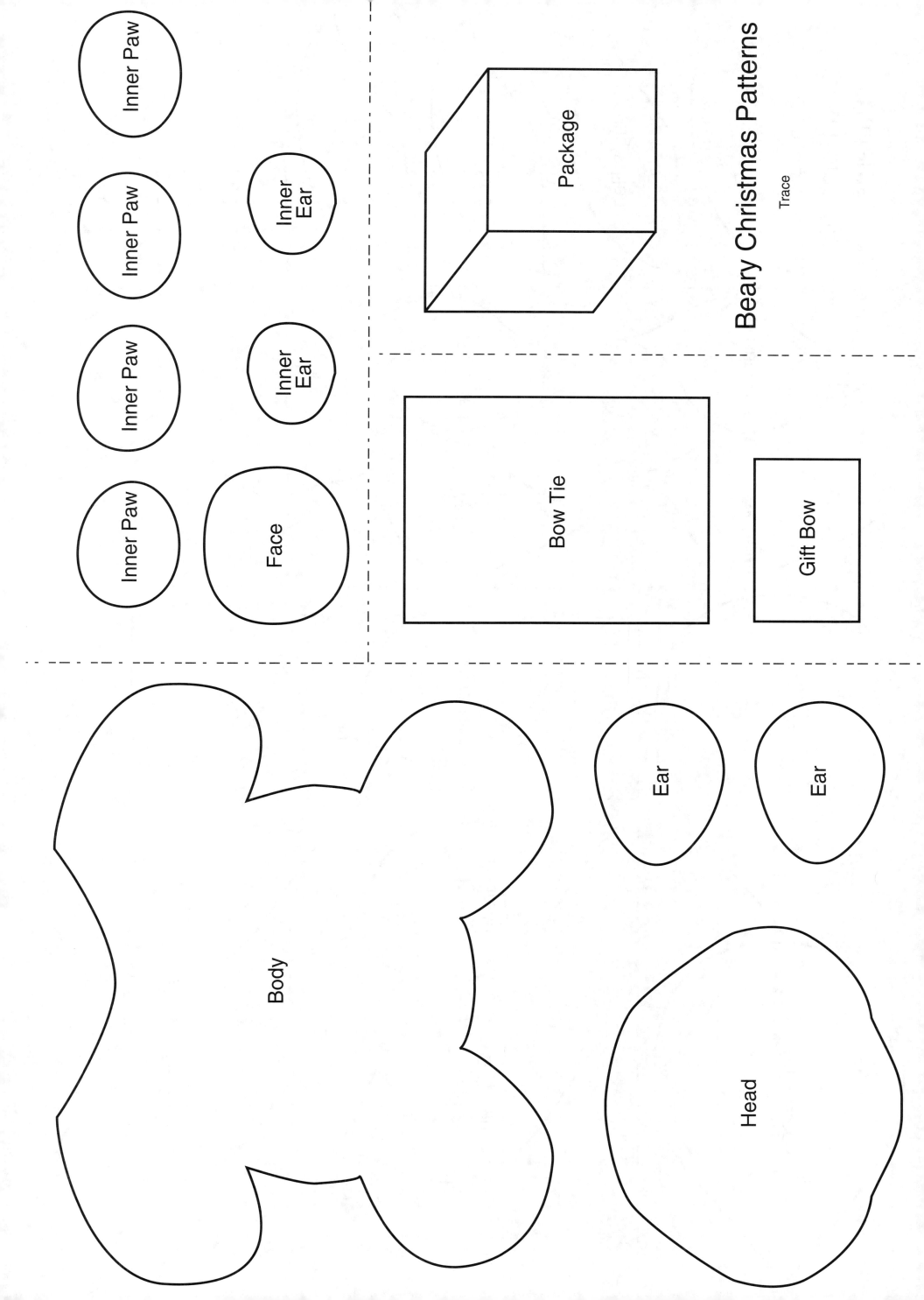

Inner Paw

Inner Paw

Inner Paw

Inner Paw

Inner Ear

Inner Ear

Face

Package

Beary Christmas Patterns

Trace

Bow Tie

Gift Bow

Body

Ear

Ear

Head

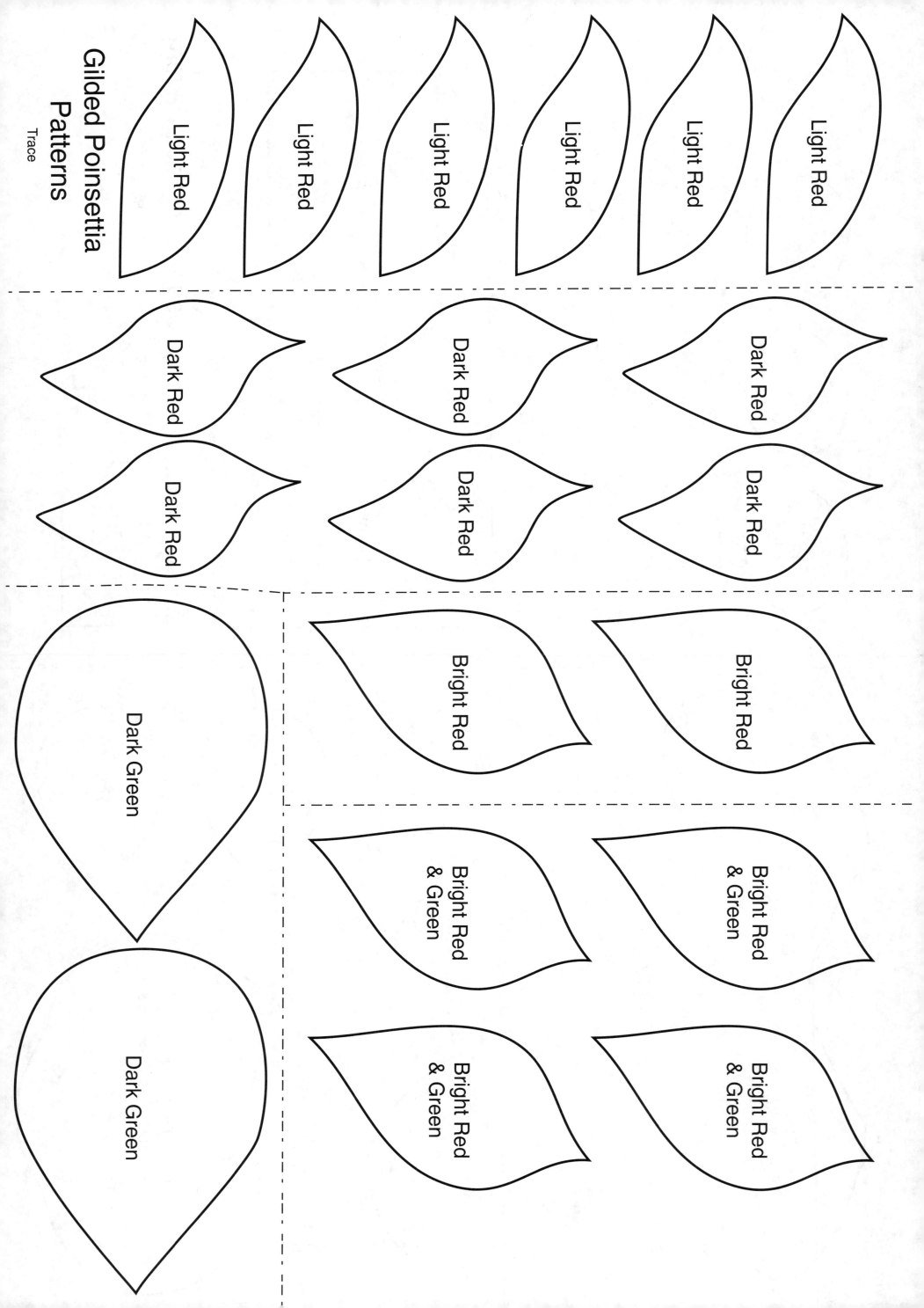

Gilded Poinsettia
Patterns

Trace

Light Red

Light Red

Light Red

Light Red

Light Red

Light Red

Dark Red

Dark Red

Dark Red

Dark Red

Dark Red

Dark Red

Dark Green

Dark Green

Bright Red

Bright Red

Bright Red
& Green

Bright Red
& Green

Bright Red
& Green

Bright Red
& Green